Dear Reader:

The book you are about to read is the latest bestseller from the St. Martin's True Crime Library, the imprint the *New York Times* calls "the leader in true crime!" Each month, we offer you a fascinating account of the latest, most sensational crime that has captured the national attention. St. Martin's is the publisher of bestselling true crime author and crime journalist Kieran Crowley, who explores the dark, deadly links between a prominent Manhattan surgeon and the disappearance of his wife fifteen years earlier in THE SURGEON'S WIFE. Suzy Spencer's BREAKING POINT guides readers through the tortuous twists and turns in the case of Andrea Yates, the Houston mother who drowned her five young children in the family's bathtub. In Edgar Award-nominated DARK DREAMS, legendary FBI profiler Roy Hazelwood and bestselling crime author Stephen G. Michaud shine light on the inner workings of America's most violent and depraved murderers. In the book you now hold, LACI, by acclaimed author Michael Fleeman, you'll take an in-depth look at the most publicized and controversial crime case in America today.

St. Martin's True Crime Library gives you the stories behind the headlines. Our authors take you right to the scene of the crime and into the minds of the most notorious murderers to show you what really makes them tick. St. Martin's True Crime Library paperbacks are better than the most terrifying thriller, because it's all true! The next time you want a crackling good read, make sure it's got the St. Martin's True Crime Library logo on the spine—you'll be up all night!

Charles E. Spicer, Jr.
Executive Editor, St. Martin's True Crime Library

On Christmas morning . . .

Scott called his parents down in San Diego. They had always been fond of Laci. She had sent his mother a heartfelt note on the first Mother's Day after they were married and signed it with her name and a happy face. His mother knew it was her son calling because she recognized his voice. But she couldn't understand him. He was crying, blubbering, incomprehensible, save for a single word.

"Laci."

Laci

INSIDE THE LACI PETERSON MURDER

MICHAEL FLEEMAN

St. Martin's Paperbacks

LACI

Copyright © 2003 by Michael Fleeman.
Update: December 2004 copyright © 2004 by Michael Fleeman.

Cover photograph of Petersons © *The Modesto Bee*/Polaris.
Background cover photograph © Reuters NewMedia Inc./Corbis.

ISBN: 0-312-99585-7
EAN: 80312-99585-0

Printed in the United States of America

St. Martin's Paperbacks edition / December 2003

10 9 8 7 6 5 4 3

PROLOGUE

At the end of the 1973 movie *American Graffiti*, a long hot night of cruising Modesto, California's downtown streets in cool '50s cars yields to an inevitable dawn and poignant goodbyes, as Richard Dreyfuss boards a prop plane for college in the East and leaves his friends—and small-town past—behind, maybe forever. The post-scripts before the credits tell us that Dreyfuss, the smart, witty, sensitive guy, goes on to become a "writer living in Canada" while the kids he grew up with in California's heartland meet less romantic fates: a tragic car crash, death in Vietnam and a career selling insurance in Modesto.

The film's director, George Lucas, was a child of that heartland town and the movie came out of his life story. The son of an office supply store owner, he went to Modesto's John Muir (elementary) School, Roosevelt Junior High School, Thomas Downey High School and Modesto Junior College. Despite his future success, he never really amounted to much academically, never ran with the cool crowd. He was short and shy and awkward. It wasn't until he became old enough to drive that he found his niche.

According to Dale Pollock's biography, *Skywalking: The Life and Films of George Lucas*, the future filmmaker "spent almost every night for four years driving up and down Modesto's streets from three o'clock in the afternoon until one o'clock in the morning. On Saturdays and Sundays he would do it all day long." Night after night, driving souped-up cars, wearing dark shades, blasting the radio, Lucas would cruise up 10th Street and down 11th Street, stopping only to hang out at the drive-in hamburger stand. Lucas would sum up his Modesto youth in the '50s and '60s this way: "Racing cars, screwing around, having fun, the endless search for girls."

While in *American Graffiti* Lucas didn't necessarily trash Modesto, which would have been an easy target, he did make it clear that the hero of the story was Dreyfuss, who, like Lucas, left the farm town for something more glamorous than selling insurance on McHenry Boulevard—just as the hero of another Lucas film left a hot dusty planet for something better in the heavens. But Modesto didn't hold this against the director, who would go on to become a major Hollywood force with *Star Wars*, and in fact has treated George Lucas like a favorite son. For fifteen years the city tried to recapture *American Graffiti*'s spirit with Graffiti Nights, an annual tradition of cruising and partying on the Saturdays after high school graduation, until the cruising and partying got so out of control (in large part due to booze and drugs) that it wasn't fun anymore. When six people were shot in 1994, the event was stopped, and the movie and its memories would be immortalized in quiet bronze in Lucas Plaza, the little park at a five-way intersection named after the director in 1997. There, cars pass a statue of a young couple, the guy in swept-back ducktail hairdo, the girl with a ponytail, sitting on the hood of a '57 Chevy.

In 1993, another graduate of Thomas Downey High School would leave Modesto for college after spending her teen years in her own *American Graffiti* way.

Only, unlike a George Lucas hero, after finding romance Laci Denise Rocha, brown-haired, brown-eyed, with a smile that would break the heart of a nation, returned to Modesto. She and husband Scott settled into a little green house on Covena Avenue to live out their years, raising children, holding dinner parties, tending to the garden, swimming in the new pool, spending time with her brother, sister, mother, father and step-father.

Her postscript was about to be written.

CHAPTER 1

"Hi, Mom."

It was Scott Peterson on the line.

Sharon Rocha was preparing Christmas Eve dinner for the family when her son-in-law called.

There was concern in his voice.

"Is Laci there?"

"No," Sharon said.

She hadn't spoken to her daughter since the night before.

"Well," said Scott, "she's missing."

The wording was peculiar.

Laci was missing. Not gone. Not out.

Then a horrible feeling overcame her.

Sharon Rocha knew immediately that something was terribly wrong.

Scott called at least two more times on the evening

of Tuesday, December 24, 2002, when a cold fog descended on Modesto.

The next time he phoned, he told his mother-in-law that he had called everybody he could think of and nobody knew where Laci was.

The third time Scott called his in-laws' house, about 6:30 p.m., his mother-in-law told her husband, Ron Grantski, to phone the police.

When the officers arrived, it took very little to convince them of the urgency of the situation. Scott hadn't seen Laci since that morning. When he got home in the late afternoon, her car was there, her purse was there, her cellular phone was there. But not Laci.

There was no note, no message on the answering machine, no word left with any family or friends. This wasn't like her. She was outgoing and bubbly, but not impetuous or irresponsible. She was the Mini–Martha Stewart to her friends, the gracious but strict hostess who served dinner at eight, and don't be late—and be sure to dress accordingly. She wrote notes for holidays and special occasions. Surely, she would have left a note if she were to leave before such an important evening.

She was the model of manners and comportment, of doing things right, of expecting the same of others.

She was also eight months pregnant—with their first child, a boy, whom they planned to name Conner.

Scott rounded up the neighbors. In the misty darkness, with temperatures dipping toward the 40s, they searched throughout his La Loma neighborhood. Scott looked distraught, scared.

Teary-eyed, he ran down Covena Avenue, past the END sign where the street dead-ended into a well-trod footpath. He went through the open gate and headed down the steep path into East La Loma Park.

She must be in the park. She had been getting ready to walk the dog.

Scott searched. The neighbors searched.

The police officers went into the park, probing the darkness with their Maglites, looking behind the bushes and rocks, walking up and down the banks of Dry Creek, searching under the footbridge. In the foggy skies, a helicopter from the Stanislaus County Sheriff's Department strafed the grounds with its powerful searchlight.

The officers roamed the streets of the La Loma neighborhood, just northeast of downtown Modesto, looking for any traces of the pregnant woman, interviewing anybody they could find, to see if they'd seen or heard anything.

They found a neighbor, Karen Servas, who hadn't seen Laci that day, but had seen her dog. At about 10:30 that morning, Servas was pulling out of her driveway onto Covena when she saw a golden retriever she recognized as McKenzie, scampering down the street, trailing a muddy leash.

She led the dog to its home at 523 Covena, where the gate to the back yard was open. That must have been how the dog got out, Servas thought. She put the dog in the yard and closed the gate and thought nothing of it until the police showed up later that evening and asked her if she had seen anything unusual that day.

By midnight, a small group of friends gathered in

front of the green house and wondered and worried:
Where could she be?

The next morning, Christmas Day, Scott called his
parents down in San Diego. They had always been fond
of Laci. She had sent his mother a heartfelt note on the
first Mother's Day after they were married and signed it
with her name and a happy face. His mother knew it was
her son calling because she recognized his voice. But
she couldn't understand him. He was crying, blubbering,
incomprehensible, save for a single word.

"Laci."

The little green house at 523 Covena sat a block and a
half from where the tree-lined street hit a fence of gray
weathered wood. The house had wood siding, a red brick
chimney, a wide driveway and wood gate that opened
to a newly installed swimming pool and patio, where
there was an outdoor chess set with marble pieces
shaped like frogs. There were young palm trees growing
next to the front window, the curtains uncharacteristi-
cally closed—Laci had liked the morning light—and a
garden of camellias, azaleas and geraniums tended by a
careful and trained hand.

At the street's end, the fence had a gap where a heavy
gate must have once swung. It was now only two thick
posts, one blackened by fire. It opened to a footpath, the
dirt worn down to a U-shaped trough a foot deep, leading down a steep embankment bordered by chain-link
fencing topped by razor wire. The path leveled to a field
of brush with green park benches and saplings braced

by posts in fields of tall green grass. The field was intersected by an asphalt bike trail lined by tall street lamps. The trail wound through groves of mature oak trees. Across the bike trail and over the field, a wooden footbridge—the floor made of planks that would make a thump-thump-thump sound as the bicyclists rode over them by day—spanned a gorge cut by Dry Creek, which wasn't dry at all, but a slowly moving stream twenty feet wide in spots, waist-deep, flowing past reeds, trees, rocks and dead branches.

It was here, in East La Loma Park, on this cold dark foggy night—Christmas Eve—that Scott Peterson, his neighbors and police searched.

He had come home, he would tell police, to an empty house and a missing wife. Her Land Rover was parked in the driveway. Her purse and phone were inside. He had last seen her at 9:30 that morning. She was working in the newly remodeled, Spanish-tiled kitchen, her sanctuary, with the TV on, the channel turned to one of her favorite shows, *Martha Stewart Living*.

She was wearing a white blouse, oversized to accommodate her pregnant belly, and dark pants. She was getting ready to walk the dog, he said, probably on the usual route, down Covena Avenue. The morning was cold and dreary, temperatures in the 50s, but feeling much colder, the fog lifting off the ponds and lakes and streams and canals and irrigated fields, shrouding the heartland of California.

Scott would tell police that he had gone outside, retrieved a couple of patio umbrellas from the back yard and put them in his new 2002 Ford F-150 pickup. Rain was in the forecast from a series of storms from the Northwest and he wanted to protect the umbrellas from the elements. He drove to a storage unit where he kept supplies from his job—he was a sales representative for California and Arizona for Tradecorp, a Madrid-based manufacturer of specialty fertilizers—and where he also kept his 14-foot Sears Gamefisher aluminum boat with the 15-horsepower outboard motor. It was a 1991 model, eleven years old—but for him it was new. He'd bought it fifteen days before from a man with his same last name, but not related. The deal was sealed on a weekend and he had returned the following Monday with the cash when the bank had opened. Scott said he'd put the umbrellas in the storage facility and took the boat out, hitching it to the pickup, then driving out of town, out of Modesto.

Scott's destination was the San Francisco Bay, eighty miles to the northwest, and if he took the most direct route, his drive would have taken him down arrow-straight Highway 132 past vineyards, fields of fragrant alfalfa, groves of almonds, dairy farms smelling of cow manure. He would have gone past Mapes Ranch, which brags on a roadside sign to be the "Home of ton bulls" and says "Breed the best and forget the rest." He would have gone over the San Joaquin River, then onto the freeway, Interstate 580, which crosses the Delta Mendota Canal and the water lifeline to Los Angeles, the California Aqueduct, before heading over the 1,009-foot-elevation Altamont Pass, where the hills are covered in power-generating windmills that look like huge propellers mounted on towers. The highway drops into the San

Francisco suburbs of Livermore and Dublin before reaching the bay cities of San Leandro, Piedmont and, finally, Berkeley. At the bottom of University Avenue, down the hill from the University of California, Berkeley, is the Berkeley Marina. There would have been little to no traffic this holiday Tuesday and the drive wouldn't have taken much more than an hour and a half.

At the north end of the marina, next to Cesar Chavez Park, and just off Spinnaker Way, is a parking lot and boat ramp. The administrative offices at the harbor were closed this Christmas Eve morning, but there was a skeleton crew on duty: two maintenance workers, a groundskeeper. A couple of them would remember seeing the Ford F-150 truck and Sears boat near the boat ramp.

He wouldn't need anybody on duty to pay the five-dollar launch fee. The fee system was automated. Five one-dollar bills placed into a yellow machine generate a business-card-sized slip of glossy paper with blue stripes down the sides informing the user: "This side up on dash." The ticket says, "Welcome to the Berkeley Marina" and provides the time and date the ticket was purchased and the time and date it expires.

The concrete ramps have floating docks on either side, and a third dock in the middle. Once in the marina, his little aluminum boat would have cruised the still waters past sailboats in their slips, then to the mouth of the harbor, where the water on this dreary morning would have been as gray as the sky and where, in all likelihood, the Golden Gate Bridge to the west, the Bay Bridge and San Francisco skyline to the south, and the Point Isabel

Regional Shoreline to the north, all would have been invisible through the fog and clouds.

Leaving the harbor, just off the left bow of the little aluminum boat, would have been an eerie bay landmark, the crumbling shell of the Berkeley Pier, jutting three miles into the bay.

He would later say that this trip to the bay was for the purposes of fishing for sturgeon, which he had been told were running. He had long been a fisherman—his earliest memories were of fishing in San Diego while his family played golf on a riverside course. His first date with his wife was on an ocean fishing boat. He was a golfer, too, and could well have hit the links at the Del Rio Country Club north of Modesto rather than go to the bay. But the plan was what it was, and he would say that he spent the better part of Christmas Eve day bobbing in San Francisco Bay in his aluminum boat trying his luck.

By late afternoon, he would tell police, he was back ashore, driving the truck, the boat behind him, making the return trip to Modesto. He placed calls on his cell phone, at least one to his wife, but he never reached her, and another to a friend named Greg Reed, who would remember hearing a voice that sounded "great." Scott wanted to make sure everybody was still on for a New Year's Eve gathering that he was looking forward to.

He returned home, he would later say, to the green house at 523 Covena Avenue in the late afternoon or early evening, just hours before he and his wife would go to her mother and stepfather's house nearby for Christmas Eve dinner. As he pulled up to the house, he saw his wife's car—the 1996 Land Rover—parked in the driveway. The house was empty.

There was a message from his father-in-law on the answering machine reminding them to bring whipping cream to the dinner. There was no message from Laci.

CHAPTER 2

It would be officially ruled a "justifiable homicide," though the man could have been shot in the back while lying asleep and it would still have been called that. That's how much the people hated Barney Garner. This was in the final decade of the 1800s, and Modesto, California, was very much a wild Western railroad boomtown. Wheat fields surrounded the community. The wheat brought prosperity, and the prosperity brought vice in the form of brothels, gambling houses, dance halls and opium dens, many of them located along the notorious Front Street. As one former mayor would recall, "Money was spent with recklessness and prodigality that baffled understanding."

The lawlessness was only appropriate, as Modesto was born out of the failure of Paradise. In 1870, when the flour-mill town of Paradise, California, refused to allow a right-of-way for the Central Pacific's San Joaquin Railroad, the rail barons bought 160 acres of wheat fields a few miles away for $3,200 and laid out a grid-pattern town next to the tracks. With industrial efficiency, the streets running parallel to the tracks were given numbers and the streets running perpendicular were given letters of the alphabet.

A station was built. Paradise was doomed.

Situated on the fertile soils of California's Central Valley, halfway between the San Francisco Bay and the peaks of the Sierra Nevada range, the newly created town was supposed to be named Ralston, after Central Pacific Railroad director and millionaire banker William Chapman Ralston, but he nixed the idea out of modesty. So this community built on an old Mexican land grant was named for the Spanish word for "modest."

Two decades later, "modesty" was the last word anyone would use to describe Barney Garner, a short, obstreperous, drunken saloonkeeper who was also Modesto's political boss, holding the town's so-called leaders—the trustees—in his rich pockets. The closest thing to an official police presence was the city marshal, who was described in a *Modesto Herald* article from 1885 as spending his days "playing poker in the various dives that curse our town, while the trustees with two exceptions are always drunk, with one exception are always dirty, and with no exceptions are always stupidly ignorant as to the welfare of the town."

The civic-minded folks banded together and elected a new marshal named Robert D. Young. One hot August night in 1890, Young confronted Garner at his Marble Palace saloon. Garner, drunk and surly, reached for his pocket, and Young solved more than a decade's worth of municipal woes with two shots from his revolver. After a loaded, half-cocked Derringer was found in Garner's pocket, the killing was given the "justifiable homicide" label.

Thanks in large part to Marshal Young's justice-by-pistol, Modesto would overcome its early growing pains to become a respectable California farm town. Just after the turn of the century, boosters held a contest to come up with a municipal motto, limited to four words. As local historian Colleen Stanley Bare whimsically notes in her book *Modesto: Then and Now*, the winner was this gem: "Nobody's Got Modesto's Goat."

Even for a farm town, this was a little too earthy, and after a public outcry the city fathers wisely went with the second-place finisher: "Water. Wealth. Contentment. Health." These are the words that now grace a 75-foot-long light-up steel arch in downtown, not far from the old railroad station, built more than ninety years ago. It's Modesto's symbol, gracing the cover of history books and Chamber of Commerce brochures.

Nearly a century later, Modesto is still defined by those four words. The canals and rivers that slice through the city irrigate the fields and groves that support the local economy. Modesto gives the world almonds, walnuts, tomatoes, beef and poultry. From its booming industrial segment, it produces the tastes of romance—Hershey's chocolates and Gallo wines—as well as the potato chips we stuff ourselves with.

Some 200,000 people now call Modesto home, and this once tiny railroad town grapples with its share of problems, from homelessness to municipal corruption. But at its core, modern Modesto still retains that early spirit. And on a dreary Christmas Day, 2002, its people fiercely refusing to let go of the search for one of their own, a homegrown girl who came back, the original, winning motto for the arch didn't seem so inappropriate.

No kidnapper—and people were convinced this was a kidnapping—would get Modesto's goat.

These early days of the search for 27-year-old Laci Rocha Peterson would be, for Modesto, both its saddest and finest hours. What began as a small search party by a few friends, her 30-year-old husband Scott Peterson and police officers grew into a crusade. Volunteers posted missing persons fliers on phone poles, utility poles and fences. Featuring a picture of Laci with her beaming smile, the posters urged people to be on the lookout for a 5-foot-1, 140-pound pregnant woman with shoulder-length brown hair, brown eyes and a sunflower tattoo on her ankle, who was last seen wearing a long-sleeved white shirt and black pants. There was a $25,000 reward for information leading to her location.

At the behest of police and volunteers, ranchers and farmers scoured their land looking for anything out of the ordinary—shoes, clothing or loose dirt. Police officers on holiday overtime pay joined firefighters in searching every inch of East La Loma Park. They walked from the El Vista Bridge over Dry Creek to Beard Brook Park. They looked for clues in the homeless encampments along the way, the transients sent running by the police invasion. Firefighters cruised Dry Creek in a rubber raft. Others waded through the shallower sections of the stream. Specially trained dogs sniffed behind rocks and trees. Cops on foot, horseback and bicycle combed the surrounding residential streets throughout the La Loma neighborhood.

As the search began, there was an eerie déjà vu. One could turn back the clock three years, to a cold Friday in February when a teen-aged girl crossing a busy street in downtown Modesto saw something on the ground on a median strip. A wallet. There was no cash left, but inside were credit cards and a driver's license.

The name on the license was Carole Sund.

In the winter of 1999, Sund, 42, and her daughter Julie, 15, both of Eureka, and Silvina Pelosso, 16, a family friend from Argentina, left a restaurant just outside Yosemite National Park after a $21.13 hamburger dinner and would never be seen alive again. An army of investigators from the FBI and state and municipal law enforcement agencies combed the rugged Sierra Nevada landscape for four days without finding any sign of the woman and the two girls or their red 1999 Pontiac Grand Prix rental car.

Then came the discovery of the wallet 100 miles away from the restaurant where they were last seen. Modesto became ground zero in the search for the missing women.

The search operations set up shop in the city. The Sund family members, including Carole's husband, Jens, a property manager, based their operation at the Holiday Inn. The FBI was stationed at the Doubletree a few blocks away. A $250,000 reward was offered—Carole Sund's parents were wealthy—and the story of the disappearances, fueled by Carole Sund's husband's emotional pleas for help, became big news.

A month later, the burned-out shell of their Grand Prix turned up in a clearing in Sonora, California, forty miles northeast of Modesto. In the trunk were the remains of Carole and the two teenagers. FBI agents went on to arrest Cary Stayner, then 37, a handyman in the motel where the three had stayed, in both their murders and also in the killing of Yosemite naturalist Joie Ruth Armstrong, 26, whose decapitated body had been found in a drainage ditch. In a jailhouse interview with television reporter Ted Rowlands, Stayner allegedly confessed to all four murders. "I did it," he reportedly said off-camera. "I'm guilty." Separate juries in separate trials agreed.

Carole Sund's parents, Francis and Carole Carrington, funneled their grief—and real estate money—into a group they created and named the Carole Sund/Carrington Memorial Reward Foundation, dedicated to helping other families of missing people by providing money and advice on dealing with the news media, as well as old-fashioned emotional support. The foundation was well capitalized. It hired as its executive director a former schoolteacher named Kim Petersen, and created a board of directors that included the Stanislaus County district attorney, Jim Brazelton, and the spokesman for the Modesto Police Department, Doug Ridenour.

The foundation was headquartered in Modesto.

It would not be long before the name Sund—and the city of Modesto—would be back in the national headlines. In May of 2001, Modesto cancer doctor Bob Levy called police in Washington, DC, when his 24-year-old daughter Chandra, an intern for the Federal Bureau of Prisons, didn't return phone messages he left for five days.

The story of the attractive missing intern from Modesto quickly became national news, fueled by whispers that when she disappeared she was having an affair with Modesto's Democratic—and very married—congressman, Gary Condit.

The Sund/Carrington Foundation and Kim Petersen came to the aid of the Levy family, publicizing a reward and helping Chandra's parents with the avalanche of media requests. The people of Modesto, a Republican district, who had backed the Democratic Condit in election after election, expressed its concern for Chandra by adorning trees with yellow ribbons. Condit would eventually admit to investigators that he'd had an affair with Chandra, but denied having anything to do with her disappearance. A sense of betrayal among Condit's longtime supporters crept across the Central Valley.

With cable news channels reporting every development in the case by day, and the pundits opining by night, the months after her disappearance became the Summer of Chandra on Fox News, MSNBC and CNN—the story was rivaled only by sensational accounts of shark attacks on swimmers.

Then, with the case still unsolved, and Condit still under a cloud, the World Trade Center fell to terrorists on September 11, 2001.

In the words of Jay Leno, "Gary Condit could have an affair and get bitten on the ass by a shark and not get into the newspapers now."

Amid scandal and an investigation, Congressman Condit's career quietly died, the nation's media focused now on terrorism. He was never charged with any crimes—nor was anybody else in Chandra's disappearance. Relentless searching turned up no sign of her, and in time the search effort ebbed, along with Condit's career, until only private investigators hired by her family were out looking.

In June 2002, investigators combing through the same Rock Creek Park that police had scoured for days found the remains of Chandra Levy. It gave her family something akin to closure—any family of a missing child will say there's no such thing as real closure—but it didn't solve the case. The discovery made big news, but the Summer of Chandra was tucked well into the pre-9/11 past. The story went away, leaving the Levy family to mourn their daughter's death and pick up the pieces of their lives quietly away from the news cameras.

Six months later, it wouldn't take a shark or a congressman to get Modesto back in the papers—just another pretty woman who turned up missing. Holidays are traditionally slow news times, when news organizations, like every other business, run on skeleton staffs and papers and newscasts lead with the same holiday-shopping stories as last year. But this story would have commanded attention on any day. It had all the elements: a pregnant woman suddenly and inexplicably disappears on Christmas Eve. A wholesome American farm town rallies around the cause to help one of its own. Family members spill emotional sound bites about how Christmas just wasn't going to be the same until Laci returned. There were great visuals. Laci Peterson's smile simply radiated off the missing persons posters.

And there was the dateline: Modesto.

Yosemite-killing central.

Condit Country.

Land of the missing women.

The reporters were right at home. They knew where to stay, where to eat, where to get their after-deadline drinks. They knew the cops. And they knew Kim Petersen and her missing persons group.

On Christmas night, the story of Laci Peterson's disappearance dominated the local newscasts on the Northern California television stations. The next morning, residents of Modesto awoke to find the story of Laci Peterson splashed on the front page of the local paper, *The Modesto Bee*. The article, which will go down as the first to mention the name Laci Peterson, was written by reporter Molly Dugan and co-written by Judy Sly, a columnist who lived near the missing woman but didn't know her.

Woman Vanishes on Walk

Modesto police and firefighters carried out a massive and futile search along Dry Creek on Wednesday for a woman who is eight months pregnant who disappeared Christmas Eve while walking her dog, McKenzie, an 8-year-old golden retriever, in East La Loma Park.

By nightfall, there was still no sign of Laci Denise Peterson, 27, who left her home on Covena Avenue about 9:30 a.m. Tuesday.

She was last seen in the park about 10 a.m. Peterson was reported missing shortly before 6 p.m. Tuesday, after her husband returned home from a fishing trip to the Bay Area, police said.

Police said they do not believe Peterson decided to leave without contacting her family.

The story went on to reveal the $25,000 reward and give details of the search, with biographical information about Laci—noting she was a local girl who had met her husband in college—and a phone number for people to call. It quoted a police official, Detective Al Brocchini, as saying, "this is completely out of character" for Laci. It also quoted one of her friends in the search, Jeff Tomlinson—whose wife Rene was planning a baby shower for Laci in a couple of weeks—as saying everybody was "choked up" over the disappearance. "She's a fun-loving girl," he said. "She's always smiling and joking with you." The article paraphrased Scott's account of returning home from the fishing trip and finding Laci gone. But there were no comments from Scott.

On Thursday, December 26, the search effort built steam, the city's spirit of resolve on overdrive. So many people came to the makeshift command center at the Petersons' little house on Covena Avenue that it had to be moved to bigger and better-equipped quarters. Brad Saltzman, manager of the nicest hotel in town, the Red Lion, who also was a friend of Laci and Scott, donated rooms, phone lines and office equipment, and quickly the hotel was buzzing with volunteers, police and a growing media contingent, including reporters from the Bay Area newspapers and television stations. Saltzman would become one of the biggest supporters of the volunteer search effort, though he was not alone. Businesses donated equipment and money for the fliers. There would be fund-raisers and prayers. Schoolchildren wore yellow and blue ribbons—yellow for hope in finding the onetime substitute teacher, blue for her unborn baby. "When you just look at her picture and see her smile, you feel the warmth and want to do something. Add to that the holidays and the fact that she's eight months pregnant," Saltzman would tell the *San Francisco Chronicle*. "Since Modesto has been through this twice before, they really just come together."

More than fifty police officers combed the neighborhoods next to East La Loma Regional Park, while eight Stanislaus County sheriff's deputies on horseback, the riders decked out in yellow slickers, went through the more rugged sections of the park grounds. Deputies in yellow life vests forded through the floating leaves and twigs in chilly Dry Creek. The Petersons' dog, McKenzie, was led through East Loma Park, but didn't take the handler anywhere. A helicopter flew overhead. Police dogs were back on the hunt. The city's public works employees lifted manhole covers in East La Loma Park.

On Friday, Day 3 of Laci's disappearance, the story hit the *San Francisco Chronicle*, which quoted police spokesman Doug Ridenour as saying how out of character it was for Laci to disappear like this. Scott's sister, Susan Peterson–Caudillo, who would become one of Scott's strongest advocates, said that if anyone had Laci, to "please let her go." As in the first *Modesto Bee* story, one grieving voice wasn't heard. "Scott Peterson," the story said, "was unavailable for comment."

The story went national as it was picked up by the wires and mentioned on the cable news shows. Audiences couldn't get enough of it. It was the right story at the right time. The country was still jittery from 9/11 and looked to be on an inevitable course toward war in Iraq. There was something about Laci's dimpled smile that touched a country looking for reasons to feel good about itself, something about her tragic plight that gave a nation something else to worry about than terrorism.

To hear their friends and family tell the media, Scott and Laci were everything that anybody would want to be.

"She has a happy, perfect life," said her lifelong friend Rene Tomlinson.

"They just seemed like the perfect couple," said her cousin Casandra Kemple.

"She was perfect for him," said Abba Imani, a Morro Bay restaurant owner who had known Scott for nearly fifteen years.

"They are just perfect," said her mother, Sharon Rocha.

That there were other things, darker things, lurking behind Laci and her marriage would be sobering revelations for another day.

For now, as Martha Stewart would say, Laci and Scott were a good thing.

CHAPTER 3

She had the smile even before she had the teeth. Laci Rocha was born on May 4, 1974, at Doctors Medical Center in Modesto, weighing in at just six pounds, with a wrinkly little face that reminded her mother, Sharon Rocha, of an old lady. As Sharon would relate to *The Modesto Bee*'s Ty Phillips in a touching profile, when she would reach for Laci in the crib after a quiet night of uninterrupted sleep, Laci would be looking up at her with a big gummy grin.

It was a smile she inherited from her mother, a fact that few would know: Sharon Rocha would rarely find reason to display it by the time the world came to know her. Pictures of Sharon in happier times show her with a grin as big as her daughter's, holding back nothing, dimples galore. One of the earliest pictures released of Laci shows a brown-haired toddler in a cute blue sundress and her mother's exact smile, so big she's baring every baby tooth she had.

It was a smile that hinted at a more devilish side. Another photo shows Laci, at age 6, in her red-and-white softball team uniform and too-big red-and-white cap, wielding a bat and flashing a grin that was as much mischief as sweetness. Growing up with big brother Brent, who was four years older, she quickly learned to hold her own. When she was 5 years old, Laci shocked the grownups by stripping off her bathing suit and jumping into the pool. It turned out she did this on a dare from her brother.

Laci and her brother spent those early years on her father's dairy farm in Escalon, a small town just north of Modesto. One family snapshot shows little Laci, maybe 1 year old, perched on a whitewashed farm fence in a white sweater, pink-and-white checkered shorts and saddle shoes. Her father, Dennis Rocha, has a protective arm around her, though she seems to be balancing just fine on her own.

Her dad cut a figure of pure farmer, circa mid-'70s— strong and tanned hands with thick fingers, weathered leather boots, faded blue jeans, plaid shirt, bushy beard and longish, unkempt hair falling out of a red baseball cap. He's squinting in the sun and has barely cracked a grin, lips pursed.

Agriculture would forever be in Laci's blood. Her mother would joke that one of Laci's earliest toys was a weed puller. Her love of adventuresome cooking also revealed itself at a young age. One of her first creations was a concoction of bananas and raw eggs.

She would always be described as a happy, perfect child, and even when things in her home life fell short of that—her parents divorced when she was 7—the family would continue to portray her life in positive terms. She would thrive in what her relatives called a "blended," not broken, family. She lived with her mother and her new step-father, Ron Grantski, in the Modesto suburbs, but also spent time with her father on the farm. If shuttling between parents ever posed a problem for Laci, nobody would ever utter a word of it in the countless interviews and press conferences that would come.

Clearly, Grantski was smitten by Laci and by all accounts treated her as one of his own. He used to call her J.J.—for Jabber Jaws—because when Laci wasn't smiling, she was talking a mile a minute.

Growing up in Modesto, Laci attended the public schools—Sonoma Elementary, La Loma Junior High, and Downey High. She grew from a cute kid to a pretty pre-teen. Weekend nights for Laci during junior high would be spent with her girlfriends at slumber parties filled with giggling, gossiping, talking about boys and listening to Neil Diamond, one of Laci's favorites. Another was Van Morrison. Her theme song would come to be "Brown Eyed Girl."

In high school, Laci joined the cheerleading squad, and after games she and her friends would meet up at somebody's house for a slumber party. During the overnights, the girls would sometimes sneak sips of champagne, but it was always girlish fun. No major hijinx, no arrests, no injuries, no vandalism or destruction that anybody would reveal.

The only thing Laci was known to wreck was a perfectly good pop song at karaoke night. What she lacked in singing skills she made up for in enthusiasm, and she was known to belt out a tone-deaf rendition of "Girls

Just Want to Have Fun" or something from the musical *Grease*.

Once, she and the girls took their fun on the road, driving down to Los Angeles to attend a taping of *The Price is Right*. Laci always set the tone: full of life. Laci and a friend once made a silly commercial, which they videotaped, with Laci holding a towel in one hand and a bar of soap in the other and shouting, "You're not fully clean unless you're Zestfully clean!"

They ran with a tight-knit group of friends—Stacy Boyers, Renee Garza and Rene Tomlinson—girls whose names would one day become familiar to those reading newspapers and watching CNN. They were second-generation *American Graffiti*, and like the hot-rod cruisers before them, they would remember those warm Modesto nights as the happiest times of their lives.

In 1993, after high school graduation, the girls went their separate ways. Laci headed to college at Cal Poly San Luis Obispo, 150 miles to the southwest, where she studied ornamental horticulture and matured gracefully from the cute slumber party cheerleader to a poised and intelligent young woman. She was president of the horticulture honor society, Pi Alpha Xi, and managed the school's plant shop. Her senior project explored the marketing of pre-wrapped bouquets. "She's a very lively person, and she's not a wallflower," one of her professors, Virginia Walter, of the horticulture and crop-science department, told *The Tribune* of San Luis Obispo. "You can't not know Laci."

But there was another project in the works that would

be far more important. As *The Modesto Bee* would later report, it was a little more than a year after she started Cal Poly that she called her mother with the news.

"Mother," she said. "I have met the man I am going to marry."

He was tall and handsome, with more than a passing resemblance to Ben Affleck—and possessing all that cocky charm. Scott Peterson came from a big family in the San Diego area, another "blended" family as Laci's relatives would say. Both his parents had three children from previous marriages and, like the Brady Bunch, this brood somehow formed a family when Lee and Jacqueline Peterson got married.

They had their own child together—Scott, born on October 24, 1972. He was the baby of the family and the joke among the seven Peterson children—five boys, two girls—was that Scott never had to walk anywhere until he was at least age 2 because somebody would always be around to carry him.

The family was active—golf, hunting, fishing. Although it would someday be his passion, Scott was slow to warm to golf. At age 6 or 7 he preferred to fish on a stream near the golf course while his other family members played. A responsible, independent boy, Scott could be trusted to be left alone with his pole until his family finished their round.

It wasn't until he was old enough to drive the cart that he caught the golf bug. At the University of San Diego High School he was a leader on the school golf team, where his teammate was future pro Phil Mickleson. After graduating, Scott's golf game earned him a partial golf scholarship to Arizona State University—but he wouldn't stay long.

Within a year he was back with his parents, this time living with them in a new home they had purchased in Morro Bay. Six months later he moved out, attended the local junior college, Cuesta College, then transferred to Cal Poly, San Luis Obispo. He was majoring in business agriculture and working two jobs to pay for tuition, one of them as a waiter at the Pacific Café, where one of his co-workers was friends with an attractive brunette ornamental horticulture major named Laci Rocha.

One day, Laci came into the café for a cup of coffee and struck up a conversation with Scott. She was so impressed with him that she gave her friend a slip of paper with her phone number and asked the friend to give it to Scott, which she did. Scott thought it was a joke and threw the paper in the trash. Later, though, he fished out the slip and called Laci.

By now, Laci had already told her mother that she had met her future husband, even though the couple had yet to go on their first date. Laci's mother asked her daughter if she was sure about Scott. Laci said she was. After Scott called, they set up a date—a deep-sea fishing trip—and it was a beautiful disaster right out of a chick flick.

Scott fell in love with Laci's beauty and spirit.

Laci got seasick and threw up.

When she recovered, she realized Scott truly was the man she would marry.

At Laci's invitation, her mother drove to Morro Bay for a weekend, and mother and daughter went to the

Pacific Café to meet Scott. He did not disappoint. As *The Modesto Bee* would report, Scott was outside waiting for them when they arrived.

"It's a pleasure to meet you, Mrs. Rocha," he said. Then, to Laci, with a smile: "Ma'am, I have your favorite table waiting for you."

They were led inside, and Scott pulled out the chairs for them as they sat down at a table with two bunches of a dozen roses, red for Laci, white for her mother.

A month later, Scott introduced Laci to his family, and the moment his mother saw the wide smile on his face she knew that this was true love. She would say that nobody had ever made her son smile so broadly.

They dated for two years. Then, on August 9, 1997, shortly after graduating from Cal Poly with a bachelor's degree, Laci Rocha, wearing a white dress and a veil cascading from a white hairband, walked down a grass carpet covered in flower petals to the strains of a string quartet toward a gazebo, where she and Scott exchanged wedding vows.

The wedding at a hotel resort at Avila Beach, not far from Morro Bay, was everything that Laci had dreamed of, down to the flower arrangements that she'd had a hand in designing. Scott was dashing in a black tuxedo and white bow tie. They had a three-tiered wedding cake decorated with pink and white roses. Friends Mike and Heather Richardson were best man and maid of honor.

After the wedding, Scott carried Laci up to their hotel room. He seemed so happy, and was laughing and shouting so much, that his brother-in-law, Ed Caudillo, who was married to Scott's sister Susan, feared that Scott was going to drop Laci.

"But," Caudillo would recall in a *People* magazine interview, "Scott had her safe in his arms."

The couple honeymooned in Tahiti, and as keepsakes they brought back seashells from their strolls on the beach. The shells would be kept for years, in a glass memento box that Jackie Peterson gave them for their wedding.

As impressed as Sharon Rocha was with Scott—his looks, his attitude, his table manners and the way he treated Laci—Jackie was absolutely thrilled to have Laci as her daughter-in-law. The following May, Laci expressed her love for Jackie in a letter.

Jackie,
　Happy Mother's Day. Your [sic] a wonderful and caring person, friend, and mother. I am fortunate to be gaining a mother in-law like yourself. Thank you for treating me like your own daughter. I love you.

It was signed, "Laci," with a drawing of a happy face.

Newly wed and newly graduated, the couple went into business together—not in one of the fields that befitted their agricultural-related degrees, but in a restaurant, operating a place in a shopping center called The Shack, a local favorite for the Cal Poly students who came in for sandwiches and hamburgers and to watch sports on the televisions.

About three years later, they sold the restaurant and moved to Laci's hometown of Modesto, living first with her mother and stepfather, then renting a place. Scott put his education to use and got a position as the California–Arizona sales representative for Tradecorp, which manufactures and distributes fertilizers. Laci would get a job as a substitute teacher for elementary school children.

In October 2000, they purchased their home, a 1,500-square-foot, three-bedroom, two-bathroom house, built in 1949 and in desperate need of Laci's eye for gardening and decorating. The house was located in the La Loma section of northeast Modesto, not far from downtown and just a block and a half away from East La Loma Park, a nice place to walk a dog or for a child to play.

It was a fixer-upper and they fixed it up right. With borrowed money, they put in a swimming pool, and Scott built a tiled deck and barbecue and refurbished the plumbing. Laci planted a garden.

Inside was the place where Laci would spend much of her time: the kitchen. It was remodeled with light pine cupboards, a sleek black electric stovetop, pots hanging from a ceiling rack and a wine rack that matched the cupboards.

The living room had burgundy-painted walls, a big brick fireplace with a white shelf for candles, a white ceiling fan, a dark antique-looking armoire for the television, a white sofa and wicker side chairs.

As she rebuilt her home, Laci also went about reestablishing her friendships from her school years, tracking down women with whom she had lost touch during college. She arranged sleepovers, just like the old days, and threw dinner parties in the green-painted dining room with windows on either side of the old-fashioned wooden table with spindle-back chairs. The parties would be the talk of her social set. Always fond of cooking, Laci went to Italy for a two-week culinary class in Tuscany to improve her skills, and in her kitchen she always kept her olive oil within reach, next to the cooktop on the green-tiled counter.

Her parties were run with Martha Stewart style, skill and precision. She expected people to be on time and dressed properly. The invitees included her friends from school years and their husbands.

Renee Garza, Rene Tomlinson and Kim McNeely all recalled those nights when they'd come into the Peterson house, mood music and aroma of food filling the air, Laci dressed beautifully in a skirt and blouse, not a hair out of place, betraying no sign of the effort that had gone into whatever elaborate meal she was preparing.

A framed slate on the wall over the Tiffany-style lamp would announce that evening's meal: the cheese-caramelized onion tortes and bacon-wrapped figs, the desserts of cakes decorated with real flowers from her garden. When she was invited to somebody else's house for dinner, manners and formality were still the rule. She'd show up in a lovely dress and heels, with an ambitious plate of food and a housewarming gift.

In the first few months in their new house in Modesto, Scott and Laci Peterson seemed to have everything—a nice home, a circle of friends, good jobs.

All they wanted now was a baby.

They had been trying for a year and a half, and while Laci wasn't panicking, she was becoming concerned. She and Scott kept going to the doctors' appointments, and kept hoping. Finally, in the summer of 2002, Laci got the good news—and so did the rest of Modesto.

An early morning pregnancy test came up positive in June 2002, and Laci worked the phone, calling friends and family to tell them of the next Peterson, due in February 2003. She was eager to find out the baby's gender so she could start decorating the nursery, and when the ultrasound test showed that the baby was a boy, Laci called her mother and said, "OK, Mom, now we can go shopping."

The parents-to-be gave the boy's nursery a nautical theme, painting the walls blue and hanging a life preserver over the crib reading, "Welcome Aboard." They hung white blinds and set up a white crib and a changing table and rocking chair, early baby shower presents from Scott's parents.

Laci loved being pregnant. At just three months, even before she was showing, she started wearing maternity clothes. She bought every maternity book she could find and watched her diet, turning down one of her favorites, sushi, because it might be bad for the baby.

Scott and Laci went to Lamaze classes at the home of their friends, Gregory and Kristen Reed, and attended prenatal yoga classes at the Village Yoga Center. They also continued to socialize. In December, Laci and Scott threw a dinner party. Then, the weekend before Christmas, the couple attended another dinner party, and Laci—seven months pregnant—arrived in a dress and high heels, handing the host a plate of crab cakes and a houseplant, according to the *Modesto Bee*.

By late December, the couple appeared to be in the perfect position to bring a baby into the world. The house was rehabbed and decorated, the nursery was ready and Scott had a good job that brought in enough money that Laci could leave her substitute teaching that month.

There was even enough money for a splurge or two. Scott bought a membership, reportedly for $25,000, to the Del Rio Country Club, a golf and tennis club north of town. He also bought himself the Sears Gamefisher boat and motor and got Laci a Louis Vuitton wallet for Christmas.

The baby, people would say, couldn't ask for better parents. Scott and Laci got along beautifully—and looked beautiful. A photo from early December had them posed in front of a Christmas tree, Laci lovely in a black dress, Scott handsome in a blue short-sleeved shirt. They walked hand-in-hand through the neighborhood like they were still newlyweds. Neighbors never heard them argue. Family members said they never disagreed over much of anything. Scott seemed to be a proud and doting husband with manners that matched Laci's exacting standards. He would always pull the chair out for her at the dinner table at restaurants. They had their separate interests, Scott with his golf and fishing, Laci with her cooking and gardening, but when they were together they seemed as one. Family members would boast that people envied the Petersons—wanted to be as happy as they were, wanted to throw dinner parties as nice as theirs were, wanted to be just like they were.

"Scott and Laci," said Laci's mother, Sharon Rocha, "are so much in love."

On Monday, December 23, two days before she was to get that wallet, Laci brought Scott into Salon Salon, the hairdresser shop where her sister Amy worked, so Amy could give him a haircut. Amy would recall that Laci was her usual bubbly self and dressed in her maternity best: black top with a floral or polka-dot print, a cream-colored scarf, a black coat and cream-colored pants.

Amy cut Scott's hair while the two sisters "hung and had fun," Amy would recall. Scott and Laci left between 7:30 and 8 p.m. and apparently went straight home, because shortly thereafter Laci spoke to her mother by phone to finalize plans for the next evening's Christmas Eve dinner. Sharon Rocha would say that Laci never mentioned anything about Scott planning to go fishing the next day, or even that he had purchased a boat.

The phone call ended about 8:30 p.m.

It was the last time Sharon would ever hear her daughter's voice.

CHAPTER 4

If Modesto was looking for a swift feel-good ending to the Laci Peterson story, it wasn't going to be satisfied. In the two days after she was reported missing, a massive search by police and volunteers turned up not even the slightest clue of what could have happened. Experts in missing persons cases always say that the first 48 hours are the most critical. The Modesto Police Department had plenty of experience investigating these cases. About 1,400 missing persons reports had come into the department in 2002 and all but a dozen were resolved, some within hours. A runaway comes home. A parent in a custody dispute turns up somewhere with the kid. The use of an ATM or credit card reveals the location of somebody fleeing work woes or a lousy relationship. Of the twelve unresolved cases, eight were clearly people who had run away—they'd either left notes or they had histories of taking off. Only two cases were completely open. One was a 32-year-old homeless woman named Rebekah Rachel Miller, last seen rummaging through trash cans in October. No clues. No witnesses. No sightings. No press. Nobody seemed to care.

The other case was Laci's.

By Thursday, December 26, there was plenty of care and plenty of concern. The reward had grown to $125,000, but this failed to bring a single credible lead. At eight months pregnant, Laci was not inconspicuous, and the TV news was now saturated with reports of her disappearance, yet nobody had come forward to say they'd seen her anywhere—not at a gas station or a store or a restaurant. Her purse was left behind, so there were no ATM or credit cards to track. Anybody she was close to was out looking for her, so there was no distant friend or relative to track down to see if she had fled there. All that searching through East La Loma Park and the streets of Modesto found no clothing, no shoeprints, no personal belongings of any kind. She hadn't called and nobody had called about her.

The weather was lousy. All the obvious places had been searched. Dismay was setting in. Police weren't ready to say she was the victim of foul play, but they were getting close.

"Somebody has her," her mother said at a press conference. "Laci would never walk away."

Sharon would step away from the microphones in tears, one of many press conferences that would end this way. A friend embraced her, and the two women cried.

As upsetting as this was to her family and friends, not to mention her new extended family—the hundreds

39

of volunteer searchers from Modesto and beyond—this was only the half of it.

In these first two days, those close to Scott and Laci had been painting that picture of perfection at 523 Covena Avenue, the sweet and lovely Laci married to the handsome and well-mannered Scott in a relationship as flawless as one of her dinner parties. There was no reason on Earth, they would tell reporters, that Laci would leave without telling anybody why—and certainly no reason to believe that the emotionally wracked Scott would have had anything to do with her disappearance.

How, then, could anybody explain the scene outside the house at 7:45 p.m. on Thursday, December 26?

It looked like a crime scene. Officers in vests emblazoned with the word "POLICE" on the back roamed the property. A big white police truck was parked in front. The night sky was ablaze with work lights, flashes from news photographers and the TV camera lights. For the next hour, until nearly 9 p.m., officers armed with a search warrant went through the green house and retrieved a number of items, including two personal computers, patio umbrellas, and both of the Petersons' vehicles, Laci's Land Rover and Scott's new Ford F-150 pickup.

That same evening, the Contra Costa Sheriff's Department brought in a bloodhound to try to detect Laci's scent and follow it as far it could. Although Scott had told police that when he last saw Laci, she was getting

ready to walk the golden retriever down Covena Avenue
to the dead end and into East La Loma Park, the bloodhound did not go that way. Rather than head north on
Covena toward the footpath, the jowly dog picked up a
scent and led its jumpsuit-clad handler in the opposite
direction, south, toward Yosemite, then to Santa Rosa
Avenue near the E. & J. Gallo Winery.

There, the dog stopped and sniffed around a Dump-
ster. Police climbed inside and peered around with flash-
lights. There was no body in there. Police wouldn't say
if they'd found anything else. Authorities did, however,
offer a theory of what the bloodhound's actions meant:
that Laci didn't walk away from her house—and likely
wasn't abducted while walking the dog toward the park
or in the park—but was driven away from her house.

The next day, December 27, police returned to the Petersons' home to search for more evidence. Officers also
went to the storage unit that Scott rented and towed away
the boat that he said he'd used for sturgeon fishing. Although bystanders could see some of what police were
taking in the searches—the cars, the boat, the umbrellas,
the computers—police refused to say officially what
they were looking for or what they had found. Behind
the scenes, police tracked down the man who'd sold
Scott the boat, Bruce Peterson—no relation—who
looked inside and found a life vest missing. Auxiliary
wheels to help launch the boat were gone and, most
interesting to police, a powdery residue was discovered
on the floor of the craft that hadn't been there when

Peterson sold it. "In the boat, on the bottom of the boat, it looked to us like it may be cement residue," Bruce Peterson told Bay Area TV station KNTV. Police immediately wondered if the residue had come from a cement anchor—and if so, where was that anchor now? It was sent out for testing, but the results weren't revealed.

But even as police kept this and other evidence to themselves, it was obvious the investigation focused from the onset on the last person to have reported seeing Laci—and the closest person in her life—her husband Scott. This was underscored by the fact that detectives also drove to Berkeley to interview people at the marina.

As unnerving as it may have been for Laci's family, not to mention for Scott, it should have come as no surprise that police were doing this.

It's a sad fact, but one backed up by a vast body of academic research, that one of the most dangerous places for a woman to be is at home with the man she loves.

According to a U.S. Department of Justice report, each year eight out of every 1,000 women could expect to be either murdered, raped, robbed or assaulted by a current or former boyfriend or husband, "intimates" in the parlance of crime research. In the case of murder, nearly a third of all women victims were slain by an intimate from 1976 to 1996, according to the report *Violence by Intimates*.

More shocking is evidence that being pregnant, as Laci was, doesn't necessarily protect a woman from murder. In fact, a 2001 study found that the single biggest cause of death among pregnant women was, in fact, homicide. The American College of Nurse-Midwives looked into the deaths of pregnant women in Washington, DC, from 1988 to 1996 and found that a startling 43 percent of them were homicide victims. A range of medical problems, from hemorrhage to infection, accounted for 47 percent of the deaths. The rest died mainly in accidents.

The study had its shortcomings—it had a limited sample by looking at only thirty pregnant women. It also didn't address the question of who'd killed the women—intimates or strangers. Yet the report painted an ominous picture: Medical science has advanced to the point that most of the health problems that used to kill women before and during childbirth have now been replaced by an affliction doctors can do nothing about—murder.

But while due diligence demanded police look at Scott, the mere suggestion that such a loving husband could have been involved in his beautiful wife's disappearance—or worse—struck the couple's friends and family as outrageous. Nobody had ever seen Scott so much as raise his voice at Laci, much less hurt her in any way. The couple were about to have a baby, and Scott seemed overjoyed by the arrival of a son.

As for Scott, nobody outside his circle of family and friends was sure what he was thinking about as the investigation began leaning his way.

Unlike members of Laci's family, Scott still wasn't talking to reporters.

But he did give a hint what was in his mind. At a

press conference on Thursday—the first day police searched his house—Scott walked out when reporters started asking about his fishing alibi.

Police spokesman Doug Ridenour would say only that police had not found any evidence of foul play and that, "At this point, he is not a suspect."

It was hardly a wholesale exoneration. But for now, that was going to have to do. And although a part of the investigation focused on Scott, it was only a part. Police were not so convinced of Scott's culpability, and apparently hadn't found any smoking-gun evidence compelling or revealing enough, to call off the missing persons search operation.

By Friday, three days after Laci had disappeared, the search expanded from the streets and park near Laci's house to the Tuolumne River Regional Park, two miles southwest of the Peterson house. Divers looked through the murky Tuolumne River waters from Modesto to the San Joaquin River.

The next day, Saturday, as rain fell, the search expanded, now covering wetlands along the San Joaquin, Tuolumne and Stanislaus rivers about ten miles west of Modesto. Police and volunteers covered the vast space on foot, horseback and motorized quad runners. In Modesto, volunteers and police officers searched the city streets—parking lots, Dumpsters, alleys, overpasses and vacant lots.

By the end of the first weekend after Laci's disappearance, more than 600 volunteers had signed up—fifty on Sunday alone—searching, questioning residents, handing out leaflets, posting fliers. Chandra Levy's mother would stop by. Gary Condit's former bodyguard, Vincent Flammini, helped search, his bulldog Noodles in tow.

It seemed that if a Modesto resident wasn't out of the house looking for Laci, they were thinking of her, hoping for her, praying for her. At the Red Lion command post, teeming with nervous energy, Modesto Police Sergeant Ron Cloward, who was coordinating the search campaign, passed out maps to volunteers designating specific areas to search and search again. A tip line was set up and calls were pouring in—340 tips by Sunday, December 29.

The search for Laci was augmented by a reward for information leading to her safe return. It started with the $25,000 posted by her family on Christmas Day, then grew during the week. Family and friends ponied up another $75,000 on Thursday, then the Carole Sund/Carrington Memorial Reward Foundation, now deeply involved in the case, with executive director Kim Petersen serving as an advisor and spokeswoman for Scott's and Laci's families, kicked in another $25,000. By Saturday, the reward hit a staggering half a million dollars due to the infusion of another $375,000 from an anonymous donor.

And still the search continued. On Monday, officials went back to the rivers and canals surrounding Modesto. The Stanislaus County Sheriff's Underwater Search and Rescue Team's frogmen swam under a section of the San Joaquin River about 15 miles from the Petersons' home alongside Highway 132, the route west of town that heads toward the Bay Area—which Scott may have taken to the marina.

The sloughs along the river and a large pond on nearby Mapes Ranch also were searched, while helicopters buzzed over the California and Hetch Hetchy aqueducts. Volunteers were assigned six blocks each to search in Modesto. The Red Lion transformed its New Year's Day Pajama Brunch into a fund-raiser, announcing it would donate all the proceeds to the search effort.

But as determined as the police and volunteers were, and as ambitious as the search campaign became, some simple sobering facts were inescapable. By Sunday, Laci had been missing five days—five days that included some of the coldest weather of the winter. Even if she had somehow escaped from her abductors and was out there somewhere, she was in deep trouble.

More difficult to accept, however, was the changing nature of the search. No longer were officers and bloodhounds poking around bushes and looking under bridges for a scared and shivering pregnant woman. The search now was covering the many canals and rivers that run parallel to or cross under the roadways out of town. The grim inference was clear: One doesn't look for a living person at the bottom of an aqueduct.

All of this was becoming hell on Laci's family. On the Friday after her disappearance, with Laci gone for three days, her increasingly frantic relatives held two press conferences to seek the public's help in finding her, and to defend Scott, who didn't attend either briefing. Laci's father, Dennis Rocha, couldn't contain his grief. "We love her so much," he said, before breaking down in tears. "Please let us have her back." Scott's father, Lee Peterson, who owns a packing company, said his son was "totally distraught and he's really tired right now. . . . It weighs on him that not only is his wife and baby gone, but that he's under suspicion." Lee even told reporters that his son had provided a Berkeley Marina launch-ramp fee receipt proving that he was there when he said he was. Scott's mother Jackie said "there's no possibility" he was involved. "They were like honeymooners even after being married five years. They doted on each other. We all wanted to be like them." Laci's mother agreed: "I think everyone envies their relationship. They are just perfect," she said. "This is just the center of her world, to have her baby and be with her husband."

Despite the searches of his home and storage unit, police were insisting this wasn't an investigation of Scott Peterson. Rather, "What we're trying to do is eliminate Scott Peterson from being a suspect," Sergeant Ron Cloward insisted on Saturday, December 28.

Trying so hard, in fact, that police had instituted the Modesto equivalent of rounding up the usual suspects. They began questioning every known sex offender and parolee with a violent past in the southeast Modesto area around the Peterson house to determine whether each had an alibi around the time of Laci's disappearance on Christmas Eve. Within days investigators had located and questioned 155 of them—and eliminated all 155 as suspects.

Police were also scrambling to handle the flood of tips into the hotline. One tip that Doug Ridenour would characterize as "credible" centered on Copeland's Sports Fitness Super Store on McHenry Avenue, a couple of miles from the Peterson house. Somebody thought they had seen Laci shopping there on Christmas Eve day, but a review of the store's security tapes turned up nothing.

A more promising lead was much closer to the Petersons' house. Susan and Rudy Medina, who lived across the street from the Petersons, had been out of town from Christmas Eve until the evening of December 26, and came home to find that their house had been burglarized. Stolen were a Tec 9mm semiautomatic handgun, a Beretta .380-caliber handgun, power tools, a camera, a Gucci watch, a Louis Vuitton purse and a safe with $3,000 in cash and $50,000 in jewelry.

Although the exact timing of the burglary wasn't known, since the Medinas were gone for almost three days, a break-in on the day they left would have occurred around the same time as Laci's disappearance.

On this quiet street, the commission of a burglary and the disappearance of a pregnant woman, all possibly on the same day and involving houses across the street from each other, seemed to be more than just a coincidence.

Of course, a break-in on either of the next two days would be meaningless in the context of Laci's disappearance except for comic relief: A December 25 or 26 scenario would mean the burglary was committed under the noses of the reporters, photographers and TV crews— not to mention a number of Modesto's police officers— camped in front of the Peterson house.

Police canvassed the neighborhood, and by Monday, December 30, had collected enough information to release a description of three people and a vehicle seen in the area of the burglary. They also offered a $1,000 reward for information leading to the arrest of the burglars.

The bounty for solving the crimes on once-sleepy Covena Avenue was now up to $501,000.

Police Chief Roy Wasden made it clear how high a priority the burglary investigation was, saying police "really feel a compelling need to get the burglary solved to see if that moves us any closer to finding Laci."

As awful as the prospect was that the two events were linked, Scott's family was clinging to the possibility the burglary investigation would help crack the missing persons case in a way that cleared Scott. "That's hopeful for us," said Scott's mother, Jackie. "Maybe she stumbled into that. Maybe they're just bad guys and not the worst of the worst."

And so the family kept that hope, insisting Scott had nothing to do with Laci's disappearance.

"No way. Absolutely not," Laci's brother, Brent Rocha, said. Brent cautioned reporters not to read too much into Scott's decision not to talk to the press. "He can't talk to the media," said Brent. "He'll break down. He's too emotional for that."

Although he wasn't doing media interviews, Scott was showing up at the search command post at the Red Lion Hotel every day, talking to volunteers, working the phones. He posted a note on one wall that summed up his feelings:

"As I see every person who comes through this door or out searching, I tell Laci about them, looking for her. Early this morning, I felt she could hear me. She thanks you."

But after a week of this—searching, hoping, praying, worrying and defending—there was still no trace of

Laci. Police made no effort to hide their darkening view of her fate. "In investigating the circumstances of her disappearance and in view of the timing of the holiday season, it becomes more apparent that her disappearance is a result of foul play," said police spokesman Ridenour. "The investigation is progressing forward with that main focus."

That night, there was a decidedly somber New Year's Eve gathering. More than 1,200 people slogged through the wet and muddy East La Loma Park and sat under cold and cloudy skies for a candlelight vigil for Laci. The strains from a women's rendition of "Amazing Grace" drifted through the gloomy night. People wore the now-familiar yellow and blue ribbons on their heavy jackets.

A flatbed trailer was driven into the park to be used as a stage. One by one, family members bared their souls for the weeping crowd, the people's faces yellow against the glow from their candles.

"Laci would be so happy to see she has so many friends and supporters," said her mother, Sharon, through tears, as she clutched red carnations. "Just keep looking for Laci. Don't give up."

The city's police chief, Roy Wasden, joined the family on the stage and pledged: "Wherever the search takes us, let's keep looking for Laci."

Laci's father walked through the crowd. "I want to meet you all," he said as he hugged people and shook their hands. "Thank you."

As for Scott, he was there, too, but he was the only member of Laci's family who didn't speak to the crowd. He also didn't sit on the stage with the family and the police chief. He was off to the side, with his 8-year-old niece, Rachael Caudillo, and her 12-year-old friend Megan Kenney, as they lit candles for Laci. At one point, he was seen meeting family and friends, speaking privately with them, and seemed to be crying.

At another point, he was seen laughing.

CHAPTER 5

While he could simply have been granting himself some much-deserved momentary relief with a friend, the sight of Scott laughing at the candlelight vigil for his missing and possibly dead pregnant wife was jarring—and only added to the questions swirling around him. While he still received support from Laci's family, who would presumably be the first to confront him if anything were amiss, Scott's seemingly aloof behavior and refusal to talk to the media caused a growing number of people to pause and wonder about what really had gone on inside the green house.

Police fueled public suspicion when, on Thursday, January 2, two days after the vigil, they held a news conference to release photos of Scott's pickup and fishing boat. "Investigators need more information to confirm or corroborate Mr. Peterson's story," Doug Ridenour said. "We want to eliminate him from this investigation. If we have an independent witness who saw him that morning, that would help." As for why Scott himself couldn't help in this regard, Ridenour said Scott was cooperating "to some degree," and that while police had not eliminated him as a suspect, "we have not eliminated a number of folks and directions at this time."

Still, police weren't releasing any pictures of any other folks' cars or boats, and as far as anybody knew, weren't serving search warrants on any other houses or storage units. The only name that surfaced at all in this investigation was Scott Peterson's.

What little exonerating evidence Scott had provided—and that the press knew about—didn't seem to impress police. That boat launch receipt that Scott had turned over "may or may not" prove he actually was fishing there, Ridenour said. At the same news conference, Chief Wasden was pounded by questions from reporters about whether this "some degree" of cooperation included Scott's taking of a lie detector test. "Polygraph would be a tool that we would incorporate in this case," said the chief. "In many crimes, you want to evaluate statements by the use of polygraphs. It's a helpful investigative tool."

He pointedly never said whether Scott had been hooked up to this helpful tool.

As the police officials spoke, investigators and searchers in the field were spinning their wheels. Tips were coming in to the hotline, but while some of them would be deemed "credible," none would blow open the case. Acting on one of the hundreds of phoned-in tips detectives showed up one day in early January at Austin's Furniture on Seventh and I streets, to inquire whether the property was being used by satanic cultists to kill babies as sacrifices, KCRA-TV of Sacramento would report. As far as owner Bill Austin knew, the only thing ever sacrificed there were high prices, and if any babies were killed for Satan, nobody had told him.

The state's Department of Justice crime lab in Ripon, just north of Modesto, announced it had received what it termed "forensic evidence" taken from Scott's vehicles and boat, but said it would take as long as a month to analyze in the serology lab. The announcement didn't specify what was being analyzed, but the serology lab typically tests biological evidence like blood, saliva or semen.

The search effort also was continuing, with officers on horseback searching the banks of the Tuolumne River just outside of town—as well as some of the waterways near the Berkeley Marina. And investigators were finishing up their questioning of the last of the city's sex offenders and parolees.

A week and a half after her disappearance, the Laci Peterson story was hotter than ever in the media, and the city—so enthusiastic in the beginning, so eager to embrace the visiting media to get out the word about Laci— was beginning to wilt under the glare of the TV lights. *Modesto Bee* columnist Judy Sly, whose name had graced the first story about the case, groused, "Laci and Scott Peterson live nearby. I don't know them, but I have seen them in the neighborhood. Some of the witnesses in this mystery are my friends. Right now, they are weary, frazzled, even scared." She noted that the news attention may help solve the case, but asked: "Does it have to come in the form of a spectacle?" To her, it was all a nasty rerun of the Chandra Levy affair. "Modesto is not the epicenter of missing women," she said. "We struggle with growth, unemployment and other things, but we are a good and decent place and that's how we want, and deserve, to be known."

Scott and Laci's families had their own struggles, worrying about Laci's fate and now, increasingly, Scott's. Once again, the families held a news conference. Once again, Scott didn't show. His father said Scott didn't have to. "He's looking for his wife," said Lee Peterson. "That's where his energies are." The families tried to keep the faith. "We feel Scott has nothing to do with the disappearance of Laci," said Sharon Rocha, who instead pleaded with the person she believed was the real kidnapper: "Have some compassion in your heart and please bring our daughter home."

Their faith would be severely tested.

On Friday, January 3—the day after police released the photos of Scott's truck and boat—the best lead in the case, and the best hope for taking the heat off Scott, seemed to go bust.

Officials announced the arrests of Steven Wayne Todd, 35, and Donald Glen Pearce, 44—two men who allegedly picked the worst possible house in Modesto to rob. A tip came in that led police to arrest the pair in the burglary of the Medina family house on Covena Avenue.

This immediately put them atop the list of suspects in the disappearance and possible murder of Laci Peterson, and Todd and Pearce just as immediately became the most cooperative burglary suspects police could ever want. Scared they would be facing charges infinitely worse than ripping off some guns and jewelry, the pair gave police the whole story—how they had been in the La Loma neighborhood before and seen that the Medina house was empty, how they then returned on December 26 at about 4 in the morning, before the sun had risen, went in through the back to avoid the news trucks parked out front, spent three and a half hours inside the house acquiring their loot and emerged after daybreak at about 7.30 a.m. Despite the presence of the media trucks, they lugged a large safe out the front door and onto the front lawn.

Police believed them. They still faced the burglary charges, but, Detective George Stough told a news conference, "We don't believe at this time there's any connection" between the hapless burglars and Laci's disappearance. Todd and Pearce later entered into plea deals; Todd pleaded guilty to felony burglary and was sentenced to 16 months in prison, while Pearce pleaded guilty to receiving stolen property, also a felony, and was sentenced to six months in jail.

This had to have come as a relief to Todd and Pearce, but was a blow to Scott Peterson's family. "I'm disappointed, I guess," his sister, Susan Peterson–Caudillo, told the *San Francisco Chronicle*. "I was a little bit hopeful."

Nearly two weeks of searching and, "We still don't have any significant leads in finding Laci Peterson," said police spokesman Ridenour. "That's unfortunate. That's discouraging."

As they had the day after Laci disappeared, police released a phone number for people to call with any information about Laci's disappearance. Then they went back to the search, again focusing on a place where Scott had been: the waters and rocky shoreline of the San Francisco Bay, where eight divers and seven dogs looked for any sign of Laci. Police said it was the improving weather, not any tip, that prompted the latest bay search.

Which all looked bad for Scott. The absence of any new leads meant the investigation circled back to him. It was starting to mount: police releasing the pictures of Scott's truck and boat, the serving of the search warrants on Scott's home and storage unit, the relentless, double-negative refrain that he had not been eliminated as a suspect, the collapse of the burglary as a viable lead and Scott's own behavior in public.

Both sides of the family were defending Scott, and still police seemed to focus on him. Surely, police knew something or they wouldn't be doing all this to such a nice young man.

Could it be possible that people were wrong about Scott—even those who thought they knew him best?

The answer was located just down Highway 99.

CHAPTER 6

From Modesto to Fresno, it's a 100-mile drive south on Highway 99. Running parallel to the Santa Fe railroad tracks, the highway goes past vineyards, fields of alfalfa, corn and tomatoes, groves of almonds and apricots, $39-a-night trucker motels, shuttered restaurants, muddy dairy farms and tall silver silos. This is the very heart of California's heartland, and the drive goes through such agricultural communities as Ceres (home of Gary Condit), Turlock, Atwater, Merced and Chowchilla (home of the 1976 kidnapping of a school bus load of children). The highway cuts through three counties, Stanislaus, Merced and Fresno, and crosses a half-dozen rivers and sloughs, including the Tuolumne, Merced, Chowchilla, Fresno and San Joaquin Rivers and the Berenda Slough that dumps out of the Berenda Reservoir just outside Chowchilla.

It could be an unnerving trip, as cars share the highway with legions of intimidating 18-wheelers jockeying back and forth from the fast to slow lane, trying to pass their brother truckers to trim a few minutes off the haul to LA. Traffic can slow abruptly and dangerously, brake lights blazing because of the snail-paced farm utility trucks, listing to one side on ancient shock absorbers. Motorcyclists zip in and out of traffic and shoot down the center line.

On a good day, if a driver doesn't get behind a truck that refuses to leave the fast lane, the drive can take ninety minutes. On a bad day, or if there's road construction, it can take much longer.

As a Tradecorp's sales representative for California and Arizona, Scott Peterson was familiar with the perils of this drive, making it frequently in his Ford F-150 pickup for his calls at farms and wholesalers in Fresno.

In all likelihood it was during one of these Modesto-to-Fresno sales calls—or perhaps under the pretext of one—that Scott met a slender 27-year-old blond massage therapist and single mom named Amber Frey.

In November 2002, one of Amber's girlfriends introduced her to Scott. According to Amber's father Ron Frey, a contractor, Amber found Scott charming, and seemed excited about starting up a relationship with him. Ron, a fiercely protective father, would repeatedly insist that Amber had had no idea that Scott was married—that the friend who'd introduced them said he was single and that Scott never said anything about a wife, much less one about to have a baby.

Amber and Scott's first date was probably a picnic, her father would recall, and the two saw each other regularly after that for the next month, with Scott making the drive down 99 once or twice a week to visit Amber, who apparently didn't see him in Modesto. They also spoke frequently by phone.

Amber had a 22-month-old daughter from a previous relationship, and Ron Frey sometimes baby-sat his granddaughter while Amber and Scott were out on a date. The child didn't seem to bother Scott. On the contrary, he picked the girl up from day care a couple of times.

Scott and Amber got along so well that on Saturday, December 14, they attended a formal Christmas party at the World Sports Café in Fresno. Young, attractive and happy, they looked like the king and queen of the winter prom. Scott wore black tux with silver tie, Amber had on a sexy red dress that left her shoulders bare. They posed for pictures at a friend's house, standing beside a pair of hanging red stockings and in front of a Christmas tree, the lit-up star shining over the heads. They both seemed open and comfortable with each other. Scott is standing behind Amber, his arms wrapped around her, his hands clasped at her waist. Amber is clutching his arm with both hands. She was so happy with the picture that she made it into Christmas cards, one of which she gave to her father, who hung it on his refrigerator.

It was shortly after Christmas when Amber was watching the news that she realized Scott wasn't all he seemed to be. The station was airing a story on the missing pregnant woman from Modesto and flashed a picture of the grieving husband.

Amber sought the help of one of her massage clients, a private investigator, and between them made a definite ID that the grieving husband and Amber's new love were one and the same.

Amber was said to be devastated.

She placed the call to the Modesto Police Department on Monday, December 30.

In hindsight, it's remarkable how early police knew about Amber. At the time, Laci had been missing for only six days, the investigation was in full swing, and to all the world the happy and loving couple were Scott and Laci, not Scott and Amber. The day that Amber called police was a busy one in the case: divers were looking in the San Joaquin River, the pond at Mapes Ranch and the nearby sloughs; detectives were reviewing the security video from Copeland's Sports Fitness Super Store to see if they could spot Laci shopping on Christmas Eve; Police Chief Roy Wasden told a news conference that he felt a "compelling need" to solve the burglary across the street from the Peterson house; detectives were interviewing sex offenders; and the Red Lion was announcing the New Year's Pajama Brunch fund-raiser.

It was the day that Doug Ridenour said police were not ruling out Scott as a suspect "at this point."

And it was a day in which Laci's family stood firmly behind Scott in the face of growing concerns about him.

Modesto police drove down to Fresno to talk to Amber. They gave her a lie-detector test and she passed. She was eliminated as a suspect.

Then she was recruited as an undercover operative.

The plan was for her to not tell Scott that she had gone to the police, so she could find out what she could about his possible involvement in Laci's disappearance, then pass that information on to police. It was going to be tricky. With the Laci Peterson story now national news, Scott had to know that it was only a matter of time before Amber found out about him and either confronted him or went to the police or Laci's family—or all of the above.

The question for police was whether Scott would try to stay in contact with Amber—and if he did, what he would say to her.

Police also had to contend with the increased press attention. It was becoming a rerun of the Chandra Levy disappearance and the Yosemite case before that. It was hard enough conducting a missing persons case in the best of times; now police had to keep Amber's involvement secret from Scott and his family, the mainstream media from the local paper to NBC's *Dateline*, and also the supermarket tabloids. *The National Enquirer* had sent at least one reporter to Modesto and there was buzz the tabloid was trying to hire a private investigator. The Condit experience proved that while the networks could throw glamour and star power at people to get information, the tabs could write checks, and there would be a great financial incentive to blow the whistle, not only for Amber, but for everybody around her who knew about the relationship with Scott.

Police knew the clock was ticking. How long could they keep Amber under wraps?

Looking back, it was impressive that they were able to sit on the biggest lead in the case for even the short time that they did. It was just one day after Amber called Modesto cops that the chief of police stood on the flatbed truck on that misty New Year's Eve candlelight vigil and faced more than a thousand people worried sick about Laci. "Let's keep looking," he said, without giving the slightest hint of what ugly developments were brewing behind the scenes. And it was on January 2—three days after she came forward—that police held the news conference to release the photos of Scott's truck and boat and announce that they were seeking help to "eliminate him from this investigation." At the time, it appeared police were turning up the pressure on Scott. Now there's one indication why. They had Amber in their corner.

Over the next five days, from January 5 to 9, the missing persons investigation and parallel body search sputtered along, with authorities finding nothing that they would reveal, but still sending strong signals that Scott remained their focus. Dogs from the California Rescue Dog Association were sent to the Berkeley Marina, where Scott said he had launched his boat the day Laci disappeared. The dogs were seen sniffing along the shoreline, and then being taken by boat to Brooks Island, just off the Richmond shoreline, where Scott had said he was fishing. Other dogs searched along the California Aqueduct and other waterways west of Modesto, along Highway 132, the most direct route from Modesto to the Bay Area and the one authorities presumed Scott had taken on his fishing excursion. Officers also peered under the Highway 132 bridge that crosses the San Joaquin River fifteen miles west of Modesto.

The search also went in the opposite direction from Modesto, to Tulloch Reservoir, 30 miles to the northwest on the way to the Stanislaus National Forest in Calaveras County. A three-day search by nine divers reaching depths of more than 100 feet under a bridge that crosses the lake found only boulders and dead trees.

The only thing that resulted from these searches, aside from a minor injury to a Tulloch Reservoir diver who ruptured an eardrum from the water pressure, was the discovery of a blue tarp in the San Francisco Bay near where Scott said he had been fishing. At first, the finding was downplayed—"It was just a tarp," said Modesto Police Sergeant Ron Cloward, who was directing the search operation—but a couple of days later police said the tarp would be examined in the crime lab.

Whether it was linked to the case or not, that was one expensive tarp. The price tag for searching for Laci and investigating the case was soaring. Two weeks of police work had cost the city of Modesto about 3,000 hours in overtime—some $100,000, the *Modesto Bee* reported. The case had consumed the full-time attention of three detectives, with another twenty-nine investigators spending at least some of their time on it. In total, some 70 officers and non-sworn police employees had been working on the case each day. And that was just the police department. The Stanislaus County Sheriff's Department had run up about 670 hours of overtime in two weeks, mainly in the search for Laci.

Police Chief Roy Wasden insisted his department would only "rev down" the investigation once it had exhausted all leads. At the time, the public didn't know that police were still aggressively pursuing the Amber Frey lead, so the rev-down was a ways off. But aside from this development, which police weren't going to reveal, there was very little left to talk about.

The searchers were searching, the investigators were investigating, and if anybody found anything, they weren't inclined to tell the media about it. On January 7, two weeks after Laci was reported missing, police spokesman Doug Ridenour announced there would be no more announcements. The daily press briefings were being discontinued. Ridenour summoned the media two days later, on Thursday, January 9, at 2:30 p.m. to hold what he called his last regular news conference. "We have run out of things to tell you," he said. "We don't have any significant leads that would put us in one direction or another."

The new no-news conference policy didn't even last the day. Within hours, Ridenour had plenty of things to tell the media.

Divers had found something at the bottom of San Francisco Bay.

CHAPTER 7

The clouds hung low over the bay and it had started to rain. The swell on the water was high. The currents ran swiftly. The forecast called for the stormy weather to get even worse. The five members of the San Mateo County Cliff/Rescue Dive Team braved the wind, the cold and the whitecaps in their boat cruising the bay at the end of the old Berkeley Pier, a rotting symbol of obsolescence.

The pier was built by the Golden Gate Ferry Company in 1926 to accommodate the exploding number of automobile drivers wanting to get from Berkeley to San Francisco. Motorists would head down University Avenue to the pier, drive far out to the deep waters of the bay, then catch a ferry to the city. It was the first ferry connection in some 50 years, and in the beginning, it was a great success. So many cars needed to get from here to there that the pier couldn't handle the traffic. On the day of the Big Game, when the University of Cali-

fornia played Stanford in football, traffic was backed up
the length of the pier and all the way up University Avenue to the western edge of the school. But the comple-
tion of the Oakland–San Francisco Bay Bridge in 1936
doomed the pier. Two years after the eight-mile-long
bridge opened, the ferry company shut down the pier
service and the pier would eventually become a platform
for anglers. The first 3,000 feet were refurbished for fishing, the rest was left to decay.

It was off the crumbling end of the pier, where Jazz
Age drivers once waited for ferries to the big city, that
Scott Peterson may have been bobbing in his little alu-
minum boat on Christmas Eve day.

And so it was here that a boatload of searchers, tossed
around by the front edge of a winter storm, explored the
muddy waters with a special sonar system and thought
they'd found something important.

The search boat was probing the depths using a side-
scan sonar, which peers through murky water by using
sound waves—technology similar to the sonogram that
expectant parents use to see their baby while it's still in
the womb. While on the bay, the boat towed a torpedo-
shaped device called a towfish. It works like a huge fish
lure slicing through the water about ten feet from the
bottom. The device emits sound waves to the side, thus
the name side-scan sonar, which hit objects and bounce
back, then get transmitted up a cable to a desktop computer in the boat. There, the computer screen displays an
image of a 120-foot section underwater. In good
weather, with a boat that's not rocking excessively—and
therefore not jerking the towfish too much—side-scan
sonar is a splendid underwater search tool. It can find

things that an underwater camera could never detect through the haze, and it's much faster, easier and cheaper than using divers.

That's in good weather. On January 9, 2003, the weather was not so good, and the boat was bouncing so much that it was all the crew members could do to keep the towfish from scraping the bottom of the bay. The images would often come back looking like a home video taken by a jittery hand.

But despite these conditions, at about 3 p.m., the search crew thought they saw something near the old pier: a little image depicting an object on the bottom in about fifteen feet of water.

An object the size of a body.

Using a global-positioning device, the exact location of the object was recorded, and divers jumped into the bay to get a look. While the side-scan sonar has its strengths, even in the best of circumstances the images that come up on the computer screen are tiny and fuzzy. A body could look like a little Pillsbury Doughboy. So could a rock. A highly trained eye can eliminate rocks and trees and such, and the scanned images are saved on disc for review later. Then, when something comes up that might be a body, as in this case, divers must go in for confirmation.

But in these early January waters, with the currents moving so strongly, the divers simply couldn't get close enough. With fatigue setting in, the weather growing worse and night about to fall, the search was called off until the weather improved.

It was a frustrating way to end the day. After more than two weeks of searching every stream, river, canal and pond in and around Modesto and the East Bay for Laci Peterson, this was as close as authorities had come to getting a break. But they had no choice. It would have been too dangerous to continue. They would be back once the weather cleared. "I'd love to put somebody in there," Sergeant Ron Cloward, who was heading the search, told the *Contra Costa Times*. "Does it make you hopeful you can bring some closure? Yes. Does it make you hopeful that there's a body down there? No." Bottom line: "I need to know what it is."

Searchers reviewed the blip on the screen and formed the opinion that it was even money that what the sonar picked up was a body.

Not 100 percent certainty, but good enough odds to rock a boat of a much different kind.

Word of the discovery was sent to police in Modesto, and just two and a half hours after telling the media that there was nothing new to report and that the daily press conferences were going to be called off for now, Doug Ridenour assembled reporters for an important announcement. He didn't want to do it, but the information had already leaked out.

"They found an object in the marina with sonar. They don't know what the object is. . . . There's a fifty–fifty chance that it is a body," he said. "We're not able to answer any questions, and I can't tell you any more."

The news hit the airwaves immediately.

Laci might have been found.

A chill fell over the family and friends of Laci and Scott, over the volunteers at the Red Lion, over the city of Modesto. Those closest to the couple tried to keep stiff upper lips. "We were told it could be just about anything," Scott's sister, Susan Peterson–Caudillo, told the *Chronicle*. She said the sooner the thing could be identified, the better. "But I know they're doing the best they can. That's all we can really ask of them. We know my brother had absolutely nothing to do with it." Scott wasn't at the search center this day. A relative said he was doing work for the fertilizer company.

The next day, the media was out in force at Berkeley Marina, even though the weather was so miserable that the search never happened. Nobody wanted to miss even the chance of witnessing this. Rumors were flying, the chaotic atmosphere intensified by an incorrect report in some editions of *The Modesto Bee* that a body had been pulled out of the bay. The report was due to wrong information from the police department, and by the time the department set the record straight, some editions had gone out. Things were so tense the Berkeley harbormaster was reluctant to send one of her boats out for more gas out of fear that the media would think the search had been launched despite the weather.

Laci's and Scott's friends and family were not part of the pack at the harbor, instead staying in Modesto at the command center at the Red Lion, where they tried to remain optimistic. Both sides of the family were united in their determination that somehow this horrific episode would come to a positive ending. "As a family we don't feel that [the] search will end up having anything to do with finding Laci," said Amy Rocha, Laci's sister.

"They're just trying to clear Scott, and they're going to have to search that area to do that. We just feel that it's been so hyped that it's going to be Laci. And we don't believe that it is."

Still, there were chinks in the emotional armor. "It has gotten harder," she acknowledged. "The days go by so quickly for us that sometimes we don't realize how long it has been."

Two days after the object was spotted, on Saturday, January 11, the weather had improved enough to resume the search of the waters off the Berkeley Pier. Before dawn, a crowd assembled on the shore, and this time it was more than just reporters, though they certainly were in force, led by the biggest name of the reporting crew, Geraldo Rivera. Nearly 100 police officers, deputies, detectives, prosecutors and various officials from a variety of agencies, from the Modesto Police Department to the Solano County Sheriff's Department, had also turned out. Anticipation ran high. Sergeant Ron Cloward said, "I just know there's an object there, and I need to know what it is."

Back in Modesto, people tried to remain calm. "We're just keeping strong," Amy Rocha told the *Chronicle*. "We're not giving up. We're going to bring her home soon." Susan Peterson–Caudillo said, "I know Laci won't be in that area."

At 6:30 a.m., just as the sun was rising, seven boats carrying divers, cops and sonar equipment left the Berkeley Marina and headed due west in the direction of the Golden Gate Bridge. Patrol boats ordered other craft—including media boats—out of the area around

71

Berkeley Pier. The search boat teams then placed buoys in the area.

At 11:45 a.m., the first diver from the Alameda County Sheriff's Dive Team went into the bay waters about 300 yards off the end of the old pier. Visibility was almost nil. The diver had to grope through the mud with his gloved hand, searching by feel, because he couldn't see anything beyond his mask.

The diver emerged from the waters, finding nothing. Then other divers went in for twenty-minute shifts. The plan was to search a swath of the bay where the sonar picked up the object. Over the course of the day a dozen divers felt around in the murky 15- to 30-foot waters.

At the volunteer command center in Modesto, people tried to keep their minds on other things, but it was difficult. Scott popped in for a while, spoke to people, then went out with other volunteers to hit the streets for the umpteenth time. Laci's brother sat for an interview with the local radio station while Susan Caudillo–Peterson looked on nervously.

Once upon a more innocent time, this had been the day set aside for Laci's baby shower, which she had planned herself, including Hershey's Kisses party favors reading, "It started with a kiss." Some of the presents had already been purchased off the registry at Babies Я Us: a Fisher-Price Deluxe Take Along Swing and a First Years Four Stage Bath System. The night before, some of Laci's friends had had a slumber party. They'd looked through old photo albums.

The next day, the women who would have been shower guests sat nervously at the command center.

It was about an hour after the divers went into the water that they believed they'd found what the sonar had detected.

The families of Scott and Laci got the word first, at around 1 p.m. Then, a little more than two hours later, Sergeant Ron Cloward made the announcement.

"We have concluded the search today of the Berkeley Marina," he said. "The dive team located an anchor sunk down in the bottom of the bay. It was not removed."

An anchor.

Imbedded in the mud.

The searchers would make more passes by the area with the side-scan sonar just to make sure there wasn't something else there. But that would be it.

A rusty anchor.

In Modesto, at the volunteer command center at the Red Lion Hotel, Susan Peterson–Caudillo's phone rang. It was a family member who had been told by police about the anchor. Scott's sister made the announcement to the center, and a cheer rose, then applause. Volunteers and family and friends embraced each other. "I had to laugh," Peterson–Caudillo said. "I just think it's really funny that it was a boat anchor. It's like—hello." While she understood that Scott was still part of the investigation, she said that "Maybe now we can move on. I would love to see efforts put in other areas."

The joy and relief was short lived. Quickly, those emotions yielded to the sad fact that Laci was still missing and nothing anybody seemed to be doing was helping to turn up any sign of her—or any clue as to how she'd disappeared. The day after the anchor incident was a Sunday, and more fliers were printed and posted, but nobody's heart was in it. Scott arrived at the center again, and again didn't talk to the media, but told some of the volunteers that the previous day's events had left him "emotionally drained." Others at the center described themselves as numb and spent.

Police returned to searching farms and orchards in Merced and San Joaquin counties, though they wouldn't say why they were there, nor would they say whether they would go back to the San Francisco Bay. Although they had tried to keep expectations in check, police were obviously feeling the sting of the affair and had started to become even more tight-lipped. "We have some specific things we are working on and places we want to look at, but we aren't going to release those locations," said Sergeant Ron Cloward at a news conference. Scott's mother Jackie continued to tell anyone who would listen that her son was feeling the pressure—a pressure that would only be relieved when the people who'd really taken Laci were found.

Unknown to the family members or to the media, police felt they knew who that person was, and they had grown tired of searching swamps and streams and the San Francisco Bay, of inconveniencing hundreds of well-meaning volunteers and running up tens of thousands of dollars in police overtime, when one word from that one person would bring it all to a merciful end.

It was time to try to strike a deal.

Prosecutors approached Scott through his attorney and made him an offer: Tell us where Laci's body is and we won't seek the death penalty.

CHAPTER 8

"Here we go! Here we go!"

The room was electric. Reporters scrambled to their seats. TV crews trained their lenses on the podium and did quick sound checks. Cable news programs interrupted their talking heads.

It was in fact time to go—time to go live and nationwide.

Modesto police spokesman Doug Ridenour walked up to the podium, which was adorned with a missing persons poster with two pictures of Laci Peterson and the $500,000 reward.

He glanced to his right toward a woman waiting in the wings. She was thin, with a long slender nose and blond hair haphazardly pinned up, with wisps falling out. She wore a black suit jacket and white blouse. A yellow ribbon was pinned on her lapel. She looked scared out of her mind.

Ridenour glanced at the crush of TV cameras and

reporters, then looked at the woman in the wings again. He nodded slightly in her direction. Then he addressed the reporters and the national TV audience.

"First of all, I want to thank you for your patience," he said, his normally strong voice, accustomed to countless briefings with reporters, now wavering. "We would like to preface the news conference by requesting that you respect our willingness to inform the media of limited information that does not compromise the investigation."

Then, he dropped the bombshell.

"Miss Amber Frey will make a brief statement and she will not answer any questions."

It was Friday, January 24, a day that would rock the Laci Peterson case.

Thirteen days had passed since the underwater search of San Francisco Bay for the object that once was thought to be a body—the search that had sent emotions flying at the volunteer center at the Red Lion. Those 13 days would be among the most intense of the investigation, when developments came faster than ever, when police began to lose some control.

Although the timing isn't certain, it was, Scott's attorneys would later contend, around this period when prosecutors approached Kirk McAllister, a Modesto-based criminal defense attorney whom Scott had hired, and presented the deal.

"An offer was made to Mr. Peterson through his lawyer in January in which the prosecution indicated it would not seek the death penalty if Mr. Peterson would provide the location of Laci Peterson's body," Scott's lawyers would later say in court papers. "Mr. Peterson, of course, did not accept the offer because he is factually innocent and did not know the location of his wife."

Police and prosecutors obviously didn't share this opinion, and while the basis for a level of suspicion so high that they would present a deal still isn't entirely clear, there are some indications of what investigators had found out—and how.

On Friday, January 10, the day after the object had been spotted by sonar in the bay, but before it had been identified as an anchor, Stanislaus County Superior Court Judge Wray Ladine decided, amid great secrecy, to authorize wiretaps on two of Scott Peterson's cellular telephones. Operating out of a "wire room," investigators were given the legal go-ahead to listen in and begin recording every telephone call that Scott made and received.

Under the law, the only limitation to the investigators' electronic eavesdropping concerned phone calls between Scott and his lawyer or members of his lawyer's staff, including private investigators. So-called privileged conversations are protected by state and federal statute, and are not for anybody else's ears. As a practical matter, the wiretap monitors have to listen to a brief portion of these calls to determine that they are, in fact, calls of a privileged nature.

This creates a delicate situation in the wire room; they can listen just long enough to make their determination, then shut off the tape recorder and turn down the volume in the wire room. They may then conduct periodic spot-checks for a few seconds at a time. But the law allows nothing more.

Go too far, listen too much, and prosecutors will have all sorts of legal hell to pay later on when they try to introduce wiretapped conversations into evidence at trial. An improper wiretap operation can doom all those recorded calls—plus any evidence obtained as a result of those calls. Play too aggressive with the wiretaps and an entire case could go down the tubes.

With all this in mind, Deputy District Attorney Rick Distaso of Stanislaus County crafted what he believed to be a strict set of rules for the monitors in the wire room consistent with the guidelines spelled out in the California Penal Code section on wiretapping.

To minimize the possibility of hearing privileged calls, the phone number of Scott's attorney Kirk McAllister was entered into the phone interception computer database, so that any calls to or from him would be electronically flagged. The wire room also had a much less high-tech method for catching McAllister's calls: his number was written on a dry eraser board.

Heading the wiretap operation was an experienced law-enforcement officer, Steven P. Jacobson, a federal agent assigned to the Stanislaus County Drug Enforcement Agency—drug cops are among those who make the most use of wiretapping in investigations—who was also a former cop for Modesto.

Despite these safeguards, attorney–client calls slipped through. One came four days into the operation, on Tuesday, January 14, while an agent named Steve Hoek was working the wire room. Attorney McAllister called Scott at 4:24 p.m. At the time, the volume was down on the speaker broadcasting Scott's calls in the room, so Hoek didn't hear the initial greeting between lawyer and client. He then heard Scott talking about his computer software, a subject of no legal pertinence to the investigation, so Hoek stopped listening and turned off the tape recorder—"minimized" the call in wiretap parlance. Hoek later came back on the line to spot-check and heard the caller ask Scott a question about the investigation.

It was then that Hoek realized that what he was hearing was a conversation between an attorney and a client. He would claim that at that moment he minimized the rest of the call and didn't do any more spot-checks.

The call apparently got by the electronic screening system because it was placed from a number not in the computer database. The monitors updated the records to include additional numbers linked to McAllister, including his home phone number and the numbers of a phone in his other office in Turlock, south of Modesto, and a secondary phone in his Modesto office.

The next day, another call between McAllister and Scott was heard, briefly, by investigators. This one came at 11:20 a.m. when the lawyer called Scott. An agent named Jesse Tovar was the monitor for the intercept, and Agent Bill Pooley was supervisor of the wire room at the time. Tovar minimized the call, then spot-checked twice to see that they were still speaking. He would say that nothing of substance got monitored, and prosecutors would later claim that for both of these calls, the initial monitoring and the spot-checking were well within legal guidelines.

Aside from what prosecutors would see as only minor

glitches, the wiretapping operation was going strong. If Scott had any clue his phones were being monitored, it didn't cut down his chat time, as he made and received hundreds of calls to or from his attorney, family members and news reporters, who were calling him incessantly. All but the conversations with his lawyer were being tape-recorded, including the stream of calls from reporters, who also were unaware they were being listened in on.

But while the wiretapping continued, another part of the investigation had hit a major snag. The *National Enquirer*'s reporters had been roaming the Central Valley for days now, and they had scored the scoop they were looking for.

They had found Amber Frey.

Police had received word that the tabloid was going to run a story about Scott's relationship with her—with photos.

Police had had her to themselves for just a little over two weeks. Now the world was going to know.

Up to this point, police had kept their knowledge of Amber secret from everybody, even Laci's family. Rather than have Laci's relatives get the cold shock of hearing about Amber from a news reporter, police decided to tell them personally.

On the evening of Wednesday, January 15, investigators sat down with Laci's family and revealed that Scott had been having an affair with a woman in the weeks before Laci's disappearance and that this woman had come forward and was cooperating with the investigation. Police also divulged that Scott had, prior to Laci's disappearance, taken out a $250,000 life insurance policy on her.

Laci's family, who had been so impressed with Scott when they first met him, who had loved him like one of their own throughout the marriage to Laci and who very publicly supported him when others were expressing doubt, were in shock. This was not the Scott they knew, or thought they knew. He had never told them about an affair. Laci had never said anything about an affair, if in fact she'd known about it, which her family was sure she hadn't. Suddenly, Laci's relatives were asking themselves: If Scott lied about this, what else was he lying about?

The only one who didn't profess to be surprised was Laci's stepfather, Ron Grantski. He would say he suspected Scott was having an affair when Scott had claimed to be out fishing in the San Francisco Bay the day that Laci was last seen. The Christmas Eve angling story didn't make much sense. A more likely scenario, he thought, was that Scott had spent the day with another woman, then cooked up the fish tale to save face. Grantski said that he even confronted Scott around the first of January, when Laci had been missing about a week, asking him if he had a girlfriend on the side. Scott denied it, and Grantski believed him.

Now Grantski, like the rest of Laci's family, didn't know what to believe.

The family didn't hold on to the information about the affair for long. The next day, a source identified in *The Modesto Bee* as a "family member" gave the newspaper the scoop, which appeared in Friday morning's editions on January 17.

Written by Ty Phillips, the story was headlined, "Relative Voices Suspicions," and recounted the police meeting with the family in which they got the disturbing revelation of Scott's affair and the insurance policy. "There were no signs," the family member told the newspaper. "They never fought. They were never abusive to each other. He's a cold and calculating type of guy."

A family source also went to a reporter for KNTV to say that the family was now having second thoughts about Scott. "The scary thing is being around him for the past weeks and him still looking for Laci," the source told the station. Similar reports on other news outlets surfaced, and soon the story had swept the nation.

Scott Peterson had been two-timing his now-missing wife.

The perfect couple suddenly weren't looking so perfect anymore.

Scott responded by doing what he hadn't done before. He talked to the media.

"I really don't care what people think of me as long as it continues to keep Laci's picture, description, tip line in the media," he told Jodi Hernandez of KNTV. "They can think anything they want of me. Let's help find Laci, that's all there is to it."

His statement was, if nothing else, weird: Hate me so we can find her.

It would get stranger. He said he planned to open a volunteer search center in Los Angeles that weekend, then another one in San Diego the weekend after that. He announced these plans even though there had been no indication from anybody—police, family or news media—of a Southern California angle to the case, save for the fact that Scott's family lived in the San Diego area.

No sooner did he say this than the whispers started: Scott needed to beat the heat in Modesto. Which was fine with him, he said. Whisper away. "Make me the biggest villain in the world if you want to," he told reporter Hernandez, "as long as it keeps her photograph in the press."

Hernandez didn't let his statements go unchallenged.

"So, you had nothing to do with this?" she asked. "I mean, people are having questions now."

"The focus is on her," Scott said. "Let's keep her picture out there. Let's keep the tip line, the description out there."

Police, meanwhile, refused to comment on the reports of the affair, and instead portrayed the investigation as business as usual, with the search effort continuing, though they wouldn't say where they were searching. Behind the scenes, it was a setback to the investigation, though not one that was unexpected. The cover was blown on one of their most important witnesses—and heaven help her.

Scoring an interview with the Other Woman would be the number-one goal of the nation's media.

At the volunteer search center, it was anything but business as usual. As the word leaked out about the affair, the center was closed—for the first time since Laci disappeared.

The next day, family spokeswoman Kim Petersen called a press conference to explain why, placing on the record what had been divulged confidentially.

"Approximately two weeks ago, Ron Grantski, Laci's stepfather, asked Scott if he had a girlfriend," Petersen said. "Scott told him no and Ron believed him. Now, however, they believe he has lied to them about this and possibly other things as well."

She didn't spell out what those "other things" were. Noting pointedly that Scott had "continually allowed family members and friends to support him personally as well as on television," Petersen made it clear how hurt the family was—and put the burden on Scott to set things right. "If Scott has nothing to hide, they ask that he prove it," she said. "The family is asking Scott to tell everything he knows and to fully cooperate with the Modesto Police Department."

The revelation of the affair placed Laci's relatives in a predicament. They didn't hide their suspicion of Scott, and yet they weren't ready to abandon hope. "The family knows that the police are doing their job. . . . They don't want to do anything that can hurt their chances of finding Laci," Petersen said. "They ask that all of you continue to search for Laci and appeal to farmers and those who live in rural areas to search their fields and barns, as well as hunters, fishermen and realtors showing empty houses."

Scott, meanwhile, was sticking to his plan to go to Los Angeles that weekend to recruit volunteers to search for Laci in Southern California. And it wouldn't stop there. He said that even though Laci's family had shut down the Red Lion Hotel volunteer center, he would return to Modesto and "open my own volunteer center and find my wife and my kid," he told KTVU-TV in Oakland in an off-camera phone interview.

He denounced the reports of an affair and the insurance policy as "a bunch of lies" that he could do nothing about but lament, "So what are you to do?"

While Laci's relatives were distancing themselves from Scott, his own family remained strongly behind him. His father told the *San Francisco Chronicle* that the allegations were "all hearsay and innuendo" and "there is no way on God's Earth Scott had anything to do with her disappearance." A bitter Lee Peterson lashed out, "I don't believe the police anymore, and I don't believe the media." When pressed on who his son may have been with in the photos, he said that Scott and Laci often attended parties and suggested the woman could have been a guest at one of them.

But no matter what Scott or his father said, it was only going from bad to worse for Scott. As his in-laws described his extramarital affair, word came out linking Scott's name with not just one missing woman case, but two.

Authorities in San Luis Obispo announced they were looking into Scott in connection with the case of a 19-year-old Cal Poly student who'd disappeared while Scott was attending the college. Kristin Smart, a freshman from Stockton, just north of Modesto, was last seen walking back to her dorm room at 2 a.m. on May 25, 1996, with another freshman named Paul Flores. She wasn't reported missing until three days later. When police looked in her room, they found her identification and other personal belongings, but no Kristin. More than six years later, she still hadn't been found.

Sheriff's investigators in San Luis Obispo, having heard about Scott's case and his history at Cal Poly, were intrigued. "We are looking at his class schedules to determine if they cross paths at all," said Sheriff's Lieutenant Steve Bolts. "We have discussed the case with Modesto detectives as well. We both are familiar with each other's case." Bolts stressed, "Scott Peterson's name has not been directly related as a witness."

Still, Scott Peterson, once the young man who could do no wrong, was now being treated in this case like the sex offenders and parolees were being treated in his wife's disappearance.

Like a usual suspect.

As the developments avalanched in—the mistress, the angry in-laws, the missing student—Scott remained under electronic phone surveillance. Not surprisingly, he was engaged in frequent conversations with his lawyer, Kirk McAllister—at least seven calls during a seventy-two-hour period. There were so many attorney–client calls it was getting to be a problem in the wiretap room.

In a secret meeting with Judge Wray Ladine to provide an update on the wiretapping operation, wire room supervisor Steven Jacobson insisted that the monitors were properly handling the attorney–client calls. Jacobson told the judge that as soon as the monitors recognized the voices of McAllister and Peterson, the tape recorder was turned off and the monitor stopped listening. Spot-checks were periodically made to see if the two were still speaking. If that was the case, the calls were minimized again. Out of what little was overheard, "No substantive information was obtained," according to the report to the judge.

Still, the judge said he "was not comfortable" with any spot-checks of calls between the lawyer and his client, and told Jacobson that agents should be off the line completely.

As he had promised the TV reporters, Scott did go to Southern California for the weekend. From the media storm up north, Scott came to Los Angeles to find a mild, sunny winter—and the first good news he had seen in weeks. On Saturday, January 18, San Luis Obispo Sheriff Patrick Hedges left a recorded statement on his media call-in-line about the case of the missing Cal Poly student. "Investigators are not looking at Scott Peterson in connection with the disappearance of Kristin Smart," the statement said. "After consulting with investigators working on the Laci Peterson case, we have determined there is no basis to shift the focus of the investigation in the Smart case." He added: "No link was established between Peterson and Smart."

Scott spent Saturday night at the home of two long-time friends, Mike and Heather Richardson, the best man and maid of honor at his wedding to Laci. The couple told *The Modesto Bee* that Scott played with their children and seemed relaxed. "We pretty much asked him if he wanted to talk about anything," said Heather Richardson. "He said, 'No,' and we pretty much let it go at that." The next day, Scott and his family, including his father, a brother and a sister, greeted volunteers at the one-day Los Angeles search center, based at the Doubletree Hotel on Wilshire Boulevard, not far from UCLA. Scott's friend Brad Saltzman, who managed the Red Lion in Modesto, had connections with the Doubletree management, and a room was made available with free coffee and cookies. The L.A. media, on this slow weekend day, were out in force, and a surprisingly large volunteer contingent showed up. About 2,000 posters were handed out.

Scott played cat-and-mouse with the reporters, pausing just long enough to explain to Fox News the need for a search center more than 300 miles away from Modesto: "We're just expanding the geographical area of the search." And his sister-in-law Janey Peterson read a statement: "Scott has our absolute and complete support and we do not believe any speculation he was involved in Laci's disappearance." His brother Joe Peterson would mingle with the reporters, reiterating the family's support and casting worried looks at his brother, who he said had tired eyes.

Not everybody was so sympathetic. The hotel received a few calls from angry people threatening to boycott the place.

Scott returned to Modesto to find even more troubles: His house had been broken into over the weekend while he was manning the Southern California volunteer center. Stolen were Laci's wedding dress and other items not identified. On Monday morning, January 20, he went jogging, then put a new padlock on his front gate. Once-quiet Covena Avenue had now seen two residential burglaries and a missing woman in the last two months. Scott told the reporters camped out front that, "Everyone is still helping look for Laci." But when asked whether he still planned to open the Modesto search center, he said he'd "be in touch."

That same morning Janey Peterson appeared on NBC's *Today* show and told Matt Lauer she wasn't convinced of the truthfulness of the reports that Scott was having an affair. "I think that we've just learned over this entire process, we just need to remain and keep our focus on bringing Laci home and return the baby," she said. "As her due date comes near, we just need to turn our focus to any circumstances that could surround delivering a baby, and that sort of thing, so our time is critical in that respect."

Lauer asked Janey if the family had confronted Scott about a possible affair as Laci's relatives had. She didn't answer directly, but suggested they had not, saying, "I feel my role is to support him and love him and be there for him and to put my primary energies into bringing Laci home safely and doing everything we can to logically do that." As for Scott's mood, she said, "As each day goes by, it does make it harder not to react to all these things that are said and these things that come up, but I think Scott has shown that he's very focused in his commitment to bring his wife and baby home."

Perhaps, but in private that focus did waver. Just hours after his sister-in-law went on national television to express her love and support for him, Scott was on the phone, not talking about bringing Laci home, but about getting the *National Enquirer* off his back. In a conversation at around 10:10 p.m., he was complaining that the tabloid had hired a private investigator to follow him. He was saying they had also tried to hire an investigator used by Scott's own lawyer.

As investigators monitored this call in the wire room, they could recognize the female voice on the other end of the line.

It was Amber Frey.

Ever since the first report of the affair and the $250,000 insurance policy, Laci's family had remained behind closed doors, declining to talk to reporters. They instead sent their spokeswoman, Kim Petersen, to deal with the press. On Wednesday, January 22, she held a news conference to announce that despite recent events the search efforts for Laci "aren't diminished at all," with the volunteer center moving from the Red Lion to the offices of the Sund/Carrington Foundation. Petersen released this quote from Laci's mother, Sharon Rocha: "I don't care about the other stuff, I just care about my daughter. I just want to find her. We just need to bring her home to us."

But by week's end the family could remain secluded no more. Police officials gave them the heads-up that Friday evening the woman who claimed to be having the relationship with Scott was going to go public.

Before the woman would have her say, Laci's family went before the microphones themselves.

The media packed the room at the Red Lion for the first face-to-face encounter with Laci's family since news of the affair. The first family member to address the reporters was Laci's sister, Amy.

It was difficult to watch.

"This past month," she stammered, "has been the most painful time I've ever experienced."

She attempted to say more, but the words were swallowed by emotion and drowned in tears. She stepped aside.

Her brother Brent then came forward. He spoke directly to his missing sister.

"Laci," he began in a trembling voice, "the last month has been the most disturbing and emotional time of my life. Your disappearance has completely changed my life as I once knew it. I miss your beautiful smile and your fun-loving personality. We talked about our children growing up together, spending summers at each other's house. Family events will be very lonely without you and Conner. Wherever you may be, I hope you know how much I love you and how important you are to me. My search for you will never end."

Brent's voice then took on an angry tone.

"Scott Peterson," he said, "did admit to me that he was having an affair with a Fresno woman. . . . I would like Scott to know that I trusted him and stood by him in the initial phases of my sister's disappearance. However, Scott has not been forthcoming with information regarding my sister's disappearance, and I am only left to question what else he may be hiding."

These were questions that Brent Rocha could only address to the media, and not to Scott directly. The rift between the families was now a chasm. "Since Scott is no longer communicating with anyone in Laci's family," Brent said, "and because we have so many questions that he has not answered, I am no longer supporting him."

Brent stepped aside.

The last to speak was Sharon Rocha. She approached the microphones and didn't say anything for a moment, trying to collect herself.

"Since Christmas Eve, our one and only focus is to find Laci and to bring her home to us," she said. "I love my daughter so much. I miss her every minute of every day. I miss listening to the excitement in her voice when she talks to me about her baby. I miss listening to her talk about her future with her husband and her baby. There are no words that can possibly describe the ache in my heart and the emptiness in my life."

Unlike her son, Sharon Rocha seemed unable to express suspicion of Scott, at least not directly—not yet, not now.

"I know that someone knows where Laci is," she said. "I'm pleading with you to please, please let her come home. You can send an anonymous letter to the police department, or make an anonymous phone call."

Later that extraordinary day, the press conference arranged by the Modesto Police Department was about anything but anonymity.

"Today," police spokesman Doug Ridenour said, "because of extensive efforts by some members of the media, Amber Frey was identified and contacted by reporters at her place of business. She notified the Modesto police about the contact. She is prepared to give a statement and she will not accept any questions."

Then, as if announcing a dinner guest, he said, "Miss Amber Frey."

She had, in fact, been tracked down that day by reporter Sontaya Rose of Fresno's KGPE Channel 47, who showed up at American Bodyworks, the massage therapy business where Amber worked. Amber wouldn't come out. Modesto police sneaked her out a back way and brought her to Fresno for the press conference.

She walked slowly to the podium, shoulders hunched forward. Wild strands of blond hair stuck out of her hastily made bun. In all the upheaval, she hadn't had time to do anything else with her appearance.

She cleared her throat, took a deep breath, sighed, and said, in a wavering voice, "OK, first of all, I met Scott Peterson on November 20, 2002."

Her head bobbed slightly as she spoke.

"I was introduced to him. I was told he was *un*married," she began, putting the emphasis on the "un."

"Scott told me he was not married," she continued. "We did have a romantic relationship. When I discovered he was involved in the Laci Peterson disappearance case, I immediately contacted the Modesto Police Department. Although I could have sold the photos of Scott and I to tabloids, I knew this was not the right thing to do. For fear of jeopardizing the case or the police investigation, I will not comment further."

She then gazed to her left and bit her lip. She was building up to something, but wasn't ready yet to say it. She looked down, sniffled, sighed, wiped her nose, inhaled and sighed again.

Then, in a shaky voice she said, "I am very sorry for

Laci's family and the pain that this has caused them and I pray for her safe return as well." Her face then showed an expression of resolve. "I would appreciate . . . my friends and acquaintances to refrain from talking about me to the media for profit," she said. "I am a single mother with a twenty-three-month-old child, and, uh, I ask you to respect my privacy. Thank you."

With that, she didn't even pause to say, "No more questions." She turned to her right and walked out quickly through a side door.

Ridenour returned to the podium. In businesslike tones in stark contrast to the raw emotion just on display, he gave the press some background.

"Amber Frey had contacted Modesto Police Department on Monday, December 30, 2002," he said. "She met with detectives and gave the information about the relationship with Scott Peterson. This information was verified by a variety of means and Amber Frey has been cooperative in the investigation and has been eliminated as a suspect in Laci Peterson's disappearance."

As for what was next for Amber, he said: "For the near future, we have asked Miss Frey not to make any statements to the media. It is her desire that you respect her privacy. Please don't follow, harass or make any other attempts to interview her during the investigation."

Then, he said: "This concludes the press conference. Just a reminder again, as we have in the past, we'll notify you if there's a significant event. We'll give you ample time to respond for a presser. I will try to answer some questions, but I'm still limited as I have been for the last month in my response."

The room erupted with questions, reporters all talking at once.

"Hold on, hold on," he said. "We'll take one question at a time, and I'll decide who. Yes."

The questions began simply enough, with a reporter asking how to spell Amber Frey's first and last name.

Then it got more pointed. This was the first time the police department had made its people available to comment on the affair. In fact, it was the first press conference of any substance since the anchor was found in the bay, and the first to address any of the criminal investigative side of the case since police had released the photos of Scott's truck and boat.

Despite Ridenour's warning that there was little he could or would say, the reporters took full advantage of this rare opportunity.

The next question came from a reporter who asked if Scott's relationship had continued even after Laci's disappearance.

"Again, that's going to be one of the areas we're not going to go into," said Ridenour, not mentioning that the relationship, to one degree or another, had continued, because Scott was speaking to Amber just days before.

Another asked if Scott had spoken to Amber on Christmas Eve.

"I don't have that information," Ridenour said.

A reporter asked how old Amber was.

"Twenty-eight years old."

Has she given the police any information that furthers your case a little bit?

"The only information that we're giving out tonight is what we already reported on, and given in this press conference," he said with exasperation in his voice. "We're not going to talk about any other information that she might be involved in as far as the investigation is concerned."

When was the last time she spoke to Scott?

"Again, we're not providing that information."

Did Scott have or not have a $250,000 life insurance policy?

"Again, that's an area we are not covering."

What made you rule her out as a suspect?

"The investigators have a variety of ways that they've been able to eliminate her from the investigation."

One reporter tried the familiar route, addressing Ridenour by his first name.

Doug, she asked, can you tell us how long they've been seeing each other?

"I can't."

Did he see her after Laci disappeared?

"We're not going to go into anything pertaining to Amber and Scott Peterson," Ridenour said, his frustration building. "We will not be discussing any part of those, other than what we talked about tonight."

A reporter pointed out that Amber had said she was introduced to Scott and "I didn't catch who introduced her."

She didn't catch it because it wasn't stated, and the spokesman didn't take the bait. "I don't remember that in her statement, either," he said. "I read it before she came out here."

Another reporter noted that Amber said she'd called police when she found out Scott was "involved" in Laci's disappearance. "Did she misspeak?" the reporter asked. "When she *saw that he was her husband*? Is that what she meant, do you know?"

It was a critical point. By saying she'd found out that Scott was "involved" in the disappearance, Amber could have been implying that he or somebody else had confided information to her that suggested he was responsible for Laci's disappearance or knew something about how she'd disappeared.

Ridenour wouldn't get into it. "Her statement, I believe, said that she did not believe, she did not know that Scott was married at the time that they had this relationship," he said. "That was her statement."

The questions continued.

Did they have any future plans? Did she talk about that?

"No, no, not that I'm aware of."

Can you characterize how helpful she has been in your investigation?

"Again, again, as we reported a minute ago, she has cooperated in the investigation. We've eliminated her from . . ."

But before he could continue, his boss, Police Chief Roy Wasden stepped up to the podium. In a voice dripping with patronizing tones, he told the reporters: "You know, we really do appreciate the media, and all the effort and attention to help us find Laci. You have been a tremendous help in getting the word out on Laci. I do believe our entire nation and possibly most of the world is aware that Laci Peterson is missing. And we want to find her. We want to find her and bring her home.

"Now," he continued, as if giving a lecture to impetuous children, "what this is starting to do is border on pretty close to being disruptive. We're not going to discuss with you the in-depth part of this investigation. We're not going to discuss with you the investigation into Laci. We're not going to discuss the relationships. We're not going to discuss where or when or how. We're giving the information that we feel we need to give and we need to give that information so that a young woman who had the courage to come forward and give us information will not be harassed as she tries to go on with her life."

The children refused to behave. The questioning resumed, with a reporter asking why police had brought her forward on this day.

"Because media people located her and were contacting her," said Wasden.

A reporter asked if she was from Fresno.

"I'm not going to discuss where she's from," he said, though he did add, "The investigation is moving forward and we will continue to move the investigation forward."

A reporter asked if Scott told detectives that he was involved with a girlfriend—or did they hear it from her?

Wasden's face showed the same frustration that Ridenour's had earlier.

"OK, let me do this one more time," he said. "We are *not* going to talk about what we have been told, we're not going to talk about what people have said. We've given the information we could give. The investigation is going to continue."

A reporter asked about Laci's family's news conference earlier in the day, when Brent Rocha said he didn't know what to believe about Scott anymore.

"Laci's family is going through a horrible time. And

you all saw Laci's family today. And they are dealing with their life as a family," he said. "I am not going to comment about Scott, this department's not going to comment about Scott. We're not going to comment about the investigation. I know it's frustrating to you. But we can't make this case a public understanding of everything that's involved. We can't do that. It wouldn't be appropriate or right. So, we're not going to talk about those things. Laci's family has information that they've decided to share. I respect that. I appreciate what they're going through, their appeal today. You heard it."

A reporter asked if the department was still focused on the search for Laci.

"That's our focus, to solve this case and get Laci home."

Another reporter asked if Amber had been cleared as a suspect.

"She's been eliminated as a suspect."

Can you tell us based on what?

"No I cannot. I won't discuss that."

Were the Rocha and Peterson families notified that she was going to come out tonight and speak publicly?

"Yes," he said.

Another reporter tried the friendly route.

"We haven't talked in a while," she said. "As far as someone backing up Scott's story that they saw him at the marina, anybody come forward yet?"

"We're just not going to go down those paths and we're not going to discuss those things," Wasden said. "The investigation has continued to move forward."

The chief said the department had received nearly 4,500 tips on the hotline, and "There are continuing information and leads as the investigation evolves that we have to follow up on. And we're doing that."

But what, a reporter asked, did that mean exactly—all this following up? The reporter asked pointedly, "Are you any closer to finding Laci now than you were the last time you briefed us?"

After deflecting question after question, the chief became surprisingly candid. "I don't believe there's a significant change that I can articulate," he said. "Are we closer? I hope so. I don't know."

Somebody asked if Scott was still considered a suspect.

"We have not eliminated Scott Peterson from this investigation," he said.

Do you know where he is now?

"I don't know."

Is this still a missing persons case?

"Yes, this is still a missing persons case."

It's not considered a homicide case?

"This is still a missing persons case. We would love to find Laci alive and well and bring her home safe."

Is the police department keeping tabs on where Scott's going?

"We're not going to discuss that."

What's her profession? a reporter asked.

"Uh, whose?" the chief asked.

Amber's.

"I'm not going to talk about that."

Has Amber had contact with Laci's family?

The chief now appeared close to wit's end.

"We're not going to discuss Amber," he said. "Amber gave you her statement. You have the information that

Amber was comfortable sharing with you. She's asked to have her privacy respected. We are going to do that. We're not going to comment about Amber, her private life, where she works, where she lives, any of those things. Amber wants to be able to go on with her life."

But the reporters pressed on.

How did Laci's family learn about Amber?

The chief sighed and said, "The question earlier was: Did we talk with the family? Yes, we talked with the family, with Laci's family."

Any more searches organized by police?

"We're continuing with the searches. We are not disclosing where those searches are. Yes, there are searches that are continuing."

And with that, Chief Roy Wasden had had enough.

"OK, we've about wound it down," he said. "There are other things I need to do and that you all need to do. I do not want to leave you frustrated and angry. I do appreciate the help you've given us. The media has been critical to this investigation in getting the word out. Thank you for your patience."

By that night, reporters had a bounty of news—comments from Laci's family, comments from the police spokesman, comments from the chief of police, and comments from the Woman Herself, Amber Frey.

Scott did not comment, and his whereabouts were unknown that Friday evening. At his parents' house in San Diego, a message to reporters from Lee Peterson was posted on the door: "We will not talk to anyone. My wife is ill. You are contributing to that. Please respect our privacy."

But on CNN's *Connie Chung Tonight*, Scott's sister-in-law Janey Peterson continued to stand behind him. She said she hadn't known about the affair until she saw the televised news conference at the same time as everybody else, but still, "It would not change what I am doing to help find Laci.

"And, to be honest," she continued, "we don't have the extra emotions and we don't have the time to chase down all these peripheries. Trusting in the Lord is all that we have."

That, and trusting in Scott.

"There is absolutely no way Scott had anything to do with Laci's disappearance," she said. "Scott's going to be OK at the end of this road, but we don't know that about Laci, and that's where our focus needs to be."

In the days after Amber's press conference, Scott seemed to find the time for at least one peripheral activity. According to Fox News, he continued to call Amber incessantly, up to six times a night, every night, from at least three cellular phones. He kept asking to see her, kept offering to buy her gifts, including a vacation she had planned. Amber, her phone tapped, and being coached by the Modesto police, turned him down.

In one call, a transcript of which was leaked to several media outlets, she asked him: "Do I need to be afraid of you?"

"Absolutely not," Scott said. "I am not a monster."

"Did you have anything to do with your wife's disappearance?"

"Ah, ah," he said, and then he paused. "No, but I know who did it and I'll tell you later when I see you."

CHAPTER 9

Despite Amber's plea for the people around her to shun reporters, it didn't take long for somebody very close to her to come forward.

One day, actually.

And it was her father.

Over the next few months, the loquacious Ron Frey would talk to everybody from Oakland television reporters to the *Globe* tabloid. Just as Scott's parents, Lee and Jaqueline, would become Scott's strongest supporters, so, too, would Ron Frey for his daughter. "I keep telling her that she didn't do anything wrong," Ron told Louis Galvan of *The Fresno Bee* in an interview from his Fresno home the day after his daughter made her public debut. "He not only fooled her, but he fooled the nation for a month."

The deception, he said, was vast, with Scott never telling her he was married and never telling her about his missing wife. He'd used his job as cover. He told

Amber that because of his travel schedule, it wouldn't be unusual for him to be away for up to a month. He even told her that he might not be around after Christmas because he was traveling to Paris.

As for Amber, Ron Frey said she wasn't in this for fame or money. "Right now," he said, "she just wants everything to go away. How do you make this go away?"

Months would pass, and it would never go away.

No matter how many interviews her father did, Amber Frey would forever be the Woman in Red wrapped in Scott's arms in that Christmas photo—or the woman in the more provocative photos that surfaced, wearing braces on her teeth and nothing else. Even her hiring of a famous LA lawyer to protect her image and interests couldn't keep the whispers at bay.

In reality, Amber Frey was, as *The Fresno Bee*'s Doug Hoagland would reveal in a detailed profile published in August 2003, much more than just the Other Woman. She was the quiet, church-going mother of a small child who tried to use her sense of humor to deal with the immense pressures of being embroiled in the Laci Peterson case.

When people would ask her, "Where do I know you from?" she would answer, "Oh, it will probably come to you."

Amber was born at County USC Medical Center in Los Angeles on February 10, 1975, to Ron and Brenda Frey, who divorced when Amber was 5. She had a sister, Ava, who was three years older, and a half-brother who became a sheriff's deputy in San Bernardino County. She grew up with both parents and seemed to move around a little within the Central Valley, attending three different high schools, two in Fresno, one in Clovis, and Fresno City College.

From one of her father's friends, a woman bodybuilder, Amber became interested in bodybuilding and fitness, *The Fresno Bee* reported. Although her choice of career would later raise eyebrows, she was actually a fully licensed massage therapist with 540 hours of training at a Fresno vocational school, and had passed the Fresno police's criminal background check for massage therapists. Her place of business was not a seedy massage parlor in the back end of town, but American Body Works, which provides therapeutic massages for injuries and sports aches.

Friends would tell *The Fresno Bee* that she had had some bad luck in the romance department even before she met Scott, living with one boyfriend who, like Scott, was also married. They lived together, but that relationship ended amid much acrimony, some of it later aired in the tabloids. Another relationship resulted in Amber getting pregnant with her daughter; the identity of the child's father has never been revealed. His name doesn't appear on the birth certificate. One man in her life, an events promoter from Fresno named Dean Hoffinger, either was or wasn't once a boyfriend, depending on who you asked.

But it was Hoffinger who played a critical role in the Peterson case; he put together the Christmas formal that Amber, wearing her red dress, attended with Scott.

Whatever his relationship with her, Hoffinger remained fond of Amber, saying that even before the Peterson storm hit, people didn't fully understand her. "She was different, but different in a good way," he told *The Fresno Bee*. "She was more cultured. It was like she didn't belong in this town."

CHAPTER 10

"In the mornings I've been taking the dog down to the park where she walked."

Scott was choked with emotion.

"It's like our time," he continued. "Laci and I's time together."

The interview with Diane Sawyer from ABC's "Good Morning America" aired on January 28 and began with this softer side of Scott. Tears. Walks through the park. Oh, how he missed Laci.

Why he felt he needed to talk, at such length, when up until now he had remained mostly behind the scenes, giving only the briefest of comments, often off-camera, will remain one of the more perplexing questions of this case. His interviews to date had not exactly gone over well. His comments about making him the villain so it'll help find Laci were strange at best. He had all but stopped cooperating with authorities.

On the morning of January 28, 2003, VCRs were running at the Modesto Police Department and the Stanislaus County District Attorney's Office, as Scott Peterson, wearing a tan suit with a big lapel button with Laci's picture on it, abandoned his right to remain silent and spoke, without a lawyer at his side, about events that could subject him to the death penalty.

"Did you murder your wife?" Sawyer asked him.

A simple no would have sufficed.

Scott rambled.

"No, no. I did not. I've absolutely nothing to do with her disappearance," Scott said. "And you use the word murder, and right now. Everyone's looking for a body. And that's the hardest thing, because that is not a possible resolution for us, and you used the word murder, and yeah, I mean, that is . . . a, a possibility. It's not one that we're ready to accept and it creeps in my mind late at night, and early in the morning, and during the day, all we can think about is the right resolutions to find her well."

It was the kind of response that makes a defense lawyer cringe—and a victim's family irate.

And it didn't stop, this train wreck of an interview. Another rambling response came when Sawyer asked Scott if he had ever hit or injured Laci.

"No, no," he said, then muttered, "My God," followed by, "No, um, violence towards women is unapproachable. It is the most disgusting act to me, um, but I know that suspicion has turned to me, and it's, uh, it's turned to me one, because I'm her husband and that's a natural thing and, um, I'll, I answer your question because of the suspicion that's been turned to me, and it turned to me because of the inappropriate romantic, um"—he drew a breath, sighed—"that I had with Amber Frey."

When he was asked what he thought he was doing with Amber, he said, "I can't answer that, I don't know."

He acknowledged it was a question that Diane should have an answer to, but she wasn't going to get it from him. He denied that he was in love with Amber, but did say he respected her, "as I imagine everyone does" from her grace under pressure at the news conference. He said there were no other Ambers out there. The relationship, he said, was "inappropriate" and "should have been brought forth by me immediately." He said he owed a "tremendous, uh, apology" to everybody.

He did claim that while he didn't tell Laci's family about the relationship, he did tell police "immediately" the first night they arrived on December 24, 2002.

More shocking, he said, "I told my wife."

He gave her the news, he said, in early December because "it was the right thing," but that it didn't destroy his marriage, although it "was not a positive, obviously."

He said they were dealing with it without arguing and that "it wasn't anything that would break us apart." Sawyer pressed him on this, but he denied there was anger. He said there was "peace with it."

So much peace, that he kept seeing Amber even after he told Laci, which he acknowledged was "definitely not the right thing."

But none of this, Scott insisted, proved he killed his

wife, although he could understand why Laci's family felt betrayed by him. "They're wonderful people," he said, but he said he'd like to be able to work with them to find Laci.

The second part of the interview began, as did the first, with Scott rhapsodizing about Laci, telling how when the two of them would be out driving the highway he would just burst into a smile and she would ask, "What the heck are you smiling about?" and he would say it was because she was there. The marriage, he said, was "glorious."

"I mean, we took care of each other very well. She was amazing," Scott then caught himself using the past tense, and added, "is amazing."

From here, Sawyer asked the tougher questions again, this time bringing Scott through the events surrounding Laci's disappearance. He repeated his story about how the last time he'd seen her she was in the kitchen with "Martha Stewart Living" on the tube, and that the blinds were closed because it was a cold winter day—not as unusual, he said, as neighbors had indicated. As for the umbrellas he was seen loading into his truck the morning that Laci disappeared, Scott said the market umbrellas—which for some reason he pointed out were eight feet in diameter "or something like that"—were headed for the warehouse because it was raining. And the reports of him taking out a $250,000 life insurance policy on Laci, he said, sounded worse than they really were. He noted that policies were taken out on both of them, that they were "an investment vehicle" and that he took them out, not that previous summer as reported, but "when we bought a home two years ago."

Finally, Sawyer asked him about "a rumor" that blood may have been found in one of Scott's cars. It was a provocative question as police had only confirmed that "forensic evidence" had been sent to the crime lab, and there had been no official mention of blood found anywhere.

Still, Scott answered it.

"I know for a fact there'll be plenty of blood in there from me," he said. "You know, I-I-I work on farms and you can take a look at my hands now and they have cuts all over them."

He even showed her his hands. "Here, you can take a look at the knuckles are always cut on me."

The Diane Sawyer interview didn't end Scott's public remarks. On Wednesday, January 29, Scott spoke from his home to Jodi Hernandez, of Bay Area TV station KNTV, saying how much he missed Laci.

"We just want her home," Scott said. "She knows how much she's loved and missed."

Hernandez asked, "You haven't given up hope?"

"No, God no. It's the only thing we have."

He repeated his brief account of the last morning he had seen Laci, saying he left around 9:30 a.m. while Laci was still in the home. "She was in a great mood. Christmas plans, Christmas Eve plans at her mom's house, Christmas Day plans here, and everything was ready, all beautiful with presents," he said. He noted that when he got back, the dog had been returned by a neighbor at 10:30 a.m. and "that's the only thing I really know."

As for the suspicion that had fallen on him, he said, "My indication is they can't rule someone out as a suspect until there's some resolution to the case."

In another interview with a local TV reporter, Scott repeated what he had told Sawyer: that he disclosed to Laci that he was having an affair. "It was the right thing to do. And, as you know, when you're not doing the right thing, it eats you up," he told Gloria Gomez of Sacramento station KOVR. "You know you feel sick to your stomach and you can't function. And you have a hard time, you know, looking at someone." Still, he insisted, "It's known. It's done. It had nothing to do with the disappearance."

And on that subject, he had a message to the real kidnapper or kidnappers: "Please take her somewhere where she can get home to us safe, just drop her off somewhere safe and go away." He added, "Every day is more and more difficult, but imagine how difficult it must be for her. So please, volunteers, do anything possible to help us."

Scott wasn't talking to everybody. *The Modesto Bee*, for instance, was on his no-comment list. "With the feelings I have about the newspaper right now, I am not interested in talking," he said, according to the paper. "The articles need to have more with Laci in them and not be focused on me."

The reviews from Scott's TV appearances came in quickly, and they were all pans. Already livid with him over the Amber revelations, his in-laws were aghast at his suggestion that Laci not only knew about the affair, but that she was dealing with it in as calm a manner as Scott suggested. If Scott were telling the truth, that meant that on the evening that Laci showed up, all smiles, at a friend's house in her high heels, holding a plate of crab crakes and a houseplant, she knew her husband was screwing around with a blonde in Fresno.

Even for somebody who put as much of an emphasis on appearances as Laci seemed to do, this would have been an Oscar-winning performance.

"I don't believe, no, I don't believe. I don't believe that was true," Sharon Rocha would later tell NBC's Katie Couric. "I'd said that before. People close to Laci would have noticed a difference in her attitude. And her personality."

What's more, Scott's in-laws struggled to believe that he would have gone fishing in the hours leading up to a big family get-together at Laci's mother's house for Christmas Eve. "I had assumed he had gone golfing because that's normally what he did was golfing," Sharon Rocha told Couric. "I'd never known him to go fishing by himself." His in-laws didn't even know he had bought the boat. "I would have thought he would have gone to play golf. That's what I was told," Laci's stepfather Ron Grantski would tell Couric. "I remember, I think he said something about that to the police that night and still thinking that that's where he went, because everybody was running around. And then he told me, Scott said then, 'No, I didn't play golf. I went fishing.' So, that was the first I'd heard of it."

The interviews also did nothing to take the police heat

off Scott, who, even as he was speaking to Gloria Gomez of KOVR, was having his phones tapped. That afternoon, at 2:04 p.m., Scott was monitored by the wiretap investigators having a phone conversation with his mother, Jackie, who asked Scott if he wanted her to pay for his "detective." He said that she could, that his name was Gary and that she should make the check out to Kirk McAllister. Thirty-one minutes later, investigators listened as a man identifying himself as Gary Ermoian called Scott to warn him that the media was outside Scott's house on Covena. The wireman—Jacobson—checked the phone number from Ermoian and found out it was listed as Gary L. Ermoian Investigations.

Amazingly, Scott would only make things worse on himself. On the same day he spoke with Gomez, he walked into Roberts Auto Sales on McHenry Avenue, and proceeded to sell his missing wife's car. Scott traded in the 1996 Land Rover against the purchase price of some macho wheels, a 2002 Dodge Ram pickup.

Scott would later have an explanation. He was making do without his own vehicle, which he'd used for work and personal use; his 2002 Ford F-150 pickup was still in police custody, having been seized as part of the search warrant on December 26.

Only he never told this to Laci's family. It took them nearly a week to figure out what had happened. The following Tuesday, they noticed a new pickup in Scott's driveway—and Laci's car gone. They spoke to Doug Roberts of Roberts Auto Sales, who explained what had gone down and who, being no dummy, promptly gave Laci's family back the Land Rover when he heard that this was all done without the Rochas' knowledge.

By now Laci's father was beside himself: First his daughter disappears, then he finds out her husband had had an affair, then the husband sells her car while she's still officially missing. "If he had any consideration for her, he would keep the car if he knew she was coming home," said Dennis Rocha.

Laci's family then got wind that Scott had looked into selling their house, which was in both his and Laci's names.

Nobody was really sure what he was trying to do. Five weeks after Laci's disappearance Scott had gone from grieving husband to heartless cad—and maybe worse.

He still had a job, but even that wasn't looking as good as it once was. When he'd returned from his Los Angeles trip, he met in his home with Tradecorp executive director Eric Van Innis, who left telling reporters that Scott had the company's "100 percent support." But now, Tradecorp was weighing its words, issuing a carefully crafted statement in legalese from a Modesto law firm.

Tradecorp has been asked to comment publicly on our company's relationship with Scott Peterson, which we consider to be a personnel issue. Our company's policy is that personnel matters are kept strictly confidential, which precludes any further comment by Tradecorp. We hope and pray for the safe return of Laci Peterson.

It looked like it would take a miraculous break to save him.

And for a brief time it looked like there would be that miracle. Somebody thought they'd seen Laci.

Alive.

CHAPTER 11

Longview, Washington, is located on the Oregon border, a long way from Modesto, California. But it was here that a grocery store clerk thought she had seen and even spoken to a pregnant woman she took to be Laci Peterson. According to a police report, the unidentified clerk was working her checkout line at the Market Place when two people walked up. One was a woman who seemed to be in her twenties, very pregnant, whom the clerk described as a "classic beauty" with sleek brown hair. With her was a man who was not a classic beauty, but a bit of a thug with "strong features" and a ruddy complexion, who appeared older than the pregnant woman.

As the clerk recounted it, the man got out of the line to pick up something he had forgotten, leaving behind the pregnant woman. The clerk told the woman that she should be wearing a coat because it was so cold that day, and the woman, remarkably, responded that she hadn't had time to bring a coat—because she had been kidnapped.

"This is serious. I was kidnapped. Call the authorities when I leave," the woman said.

Then the ruddy-complexioned man came back to the line and asked the two women what they were talking about.

"She said you kidnapped her," the clerk said.

This got the man angry, so the clerk tried to defuse the situation by jokingly telling the man that her own husband had kidnapped her for a dinner date. Her kidding seemed to work because the man started laughing, saying, "Yeah, I guess I kidnapped her."

The pair walked out, and the clerk recalled trying to find a phone book to call police. She couldn't find the book. Then, in a statement that defied credibility, she said she became distracted and forgot about the pregnant kidnap victim until the clerk happened to be watching CNN one day, saw something on the Laci Peterson case and realized that Laci could have been the woman she'd seen in the store.

Longview police then reported the incident to Modesto police. The store had a security video, and Longview authorities said they were in the process of going through the tapes to see if anything even vaguely matching the events described by the clerk had happened.

It would mean another tense night of waiting and wondering, only this time expectations were tempered by painful experience. The anchor discovery had taught Laci's family to keep their emotions in check. And it was a good thing they did, for the next day, Friday,

January 31, Bob Burgreen, the chief of police for Long-view, issued this statement:

"Our hearts go out to the family of Laci Peterson. We had hoped that this could possibly be a breakthrough lead, but now we believe that is not the case."

A review of forty-five hours of security video turned up no sign of Laci Peterson. There was no cheer among volunteers, no cries of joy. Everyone had learned their lesson the last time.

"It didn't make sense from the beginning," family spokeswoman Kim Petersen said. "I mean, how many times does a pregnant woman walk into a store and say she's been kidnapped? How could you forget something like that?"

By that night, whether it was a reaction to yet another false alarm, or just his growing anger and frustration, Laci's stepfather Ron Grantski seemed to be boiling. Her family had posted a message on their Web site announcing another candlelight vigil for the evening. "Light a candle, say a prayer or think a positive thought for [her] return," the message said. "No particular faith is endorsed. Some will light candles to St. Jude, Holy Mary. Others will just light a plain candle, leave a porch light on or will stop for a moment of silence to send their positive prayer into the world."

Dozens of people stopped in front of the Grantski house at 7 p.m., candles in hand, prayers in their hearts. But when Grantski came out to join them, he wasn't in the mood for anything positive.

He said he wanted Laci back.

Now.

The word he used to describe the person who took her was "monster."

Five days later, Grantski was still hot. On Wednesday, February 5, Laci's family held a news conference in La Loma Park—the first time the family had addressed the press together since the day Amber Frey went public— to announce they would launch another round of searches.

Although they didn't say it, the family implied that they had accepted that Laci was dead. The first search was set for the Delta–Mendota Canal. Scott wasn't at this press conference, of course. In fact, nobody was sure where he was.

There were rumors he was out of the country, attending a U.S. Grains Council conference set for that Sunday, February 2, through Wednesday, February 5, at the Hilton hotel in Guadalajara, Mexico. A delegation from his company had reserved rooms.

Laci's stepfather made it clear that wherever Scott was, he had better get back.

"He has said since the first night he wanted the focus on finding Laci, not on him," said Grantski. "Well, with the things he's been doing and saying, the focus is all on him. You want to change the focus, Scott, talk to the Modesto police. End this circus."

CHAPTER 12

Laci Peterson was to have given birth to her son Conner on Monday, February 10, 2003. Instead, on this day a couple of dozen friends and family members bundled up in sweaters and coats and headed for the place they had first looked for her that damp winter night, East La Loma Park. Over the sounds of quiet weeping, a recording of the pop song "I'm With You" by Avril Lavigne wafted through the park, a song that seemed written for Laci, as Avril sang about a girl standing on a bridge, waiting in the dark on a "damn cold night," wondering if anyone was trying to find her.

After the tumultuous events of the previous weeks, the candlelight vigil served as a quiet reminder of what, and who, this case was all about. It was also a reminder of how important the plight of Laci and her unborn child had become to the nation.

Joining the two dozen people at the vigil were another

two dozen reporters and camera crew members.

Once again, Scott didn't show up, although by now people knew where he was: at his home on Covena Avenue, where a sign outside on the lawn still advertised the half-million-dollar reward for information that Scott's growing legions of detractors thought he alone possessed. He had done his media interviews and was lying low. He hadn't been arrested, but he hadn't been cleared, either. He was neither suspected nor eliminated.

Police spokesman Doug Ridenour would knock down the latest report that an arrest was "imminent," yet on another day a pair of detectives were seen visiting Scott in his house. His in-laws were distancing themselves from him. The pundits were all over him on TV for his interviews. His in-laws turned up their rhetoric, still sore that he'd sold Laci's car and was inquiring about selling their house. "You pile all that stuff together and it just makes you question what's really going on," said Laci's brother Brent Rocha. "His behavior is obviously not reflecting one that has a missing wife."

Even the local vandals weren't sparing Scott. Already, somebody had broken into his house when he was in Los Angeles for the weekend, then a couple of weeks later, somebody smashed in the door of his storage unit. Nothing was taken because there was nothing left to take. What police hadn't seized with a search warrant, Scott had removed himself. On the night of the candlelight vigil in the park, he lamented to a KTXL-TV reporter: "It's hard to go on."

Scott did, however, have the support of his own family. They tried to explain at least some of Scott's actions:

Scott Peterson
(AP/Wide World
Photos)

The home in Modesto, CA, where Scott and Laci Peterson made
their life together. (Michael Fleeman)

Modesto Police Department Detective Doug Ridenour addresses reporters outside Scott and Laci's home. (AP/Wide World Photos)

The Shack restaurant, which Scott and Laci operated after they married. (Michael Fleeman)

Berkeley Marina on San Francisco Bay. Scott told the world that he had come here on December 24, 2002, to get a little fishing in before Christmas Eve dinner. (Michael Fleeman)

VOLUNTEERS

AS I SEE EVERY PERSON COME THROUGH THIS DOOR, OR OUT SEARCHING, I TELL LACI ABOUT THEM, LOOKING FOR HER.

EARLY THIS MORNING I FELT SHE COULD HEAR ME SHE THANKS YOU.

LACI'S HUSBAND

In the early stages of the search for Laci Peterson, Scott appeared a deeply concerned husband, but his behavior would turn erratic as secrets from his past emerged. (Both: AP/Wide World Photos)

Amber Frey, of Fresno, CA, revealed that she and Scott had been having a love affair at the time of Laci's disappearance. (AP/Wide World Photos)

Frey's attorney, Gloria Allred, addressing the press. (Michael Fleeman)

Laci's mother, Sharon Rocha, and her stepfather, Ron Grantski. (AP/Wide World Photos)

Laci's sister, Amy Rocha. (AP/Wide World Photos)

Scott Peterson, as he appeared at the time of his arrest. Reports suggested he was carrying his brother's ID and $10,000 in cash. (AP/Wide World Photos)

Scott's parents, Jackie and Lee Peterson, loved Laci like a daughter—and stuck by their son. (AP/Wide World Photos)

Police divers searched for Laci's body in the cold waters off Berkeley. It would wash ashore in April 2003. (AP/Wide World Photos)

Deputy District Attorney John Goold, spokesman for the prosecution, discussing Scott Peterson's case with reporters. (Michael Fleeman)

After a reporter overheard a conversation between members of Scott Peterson's defense team, attention focused on this so-called "Satanic art" a couple of miles from where Laci's body was found. The defense floated the theory a cult was responsible for Laci's death. (Both: Michael Fleeman)

After authorities confirmed Laci Peterson's body had been found, mourners grieved in the front yard of the home she so loved. Others lashed out at her accused killer. (Both: AP/Wide World Photos)

Kim Petersen—no relation to Scott—was the spokeswoman for Laci's parents and siblings. (AP/Wide World Photos)

The media, back in Condit County, now obsessed with the Peterson case. (Michael Fleeman)

Scott Peterson seated next to his attorney, Mark Geragos. (AP/Wide World Photos)

Jackie and Lee Peterson at the Stanislaus County Courthouse. (Michael Fleeman)

Sharon Rocha, mother of Laci Peterson, who would have been Conner's grandmother—at their memorial service. (AP/Wide World Photos)

he'd sold the car, they said, because the couple had long decided to buy what they considered a safer car for the baby. As for contacting real estate agents, they said Scott was looking into the possibility of getting another house once Laci was found.

And Scott's family insisted she could still be found. His mother and father joined Scott's siblings at a news conference in San Diego on Thursday, February 13, to show that, despite everything that had been said, they weren't going to give up looking for Laci.

By now, the family showed how media-versed it had become, opening the press conference like veteran publicists. Scott's sister, Susan Peterson–Caudillo, identified herself and spelled her name, then instructed the reporters: "We're going to be reading one short statement. We won't be taking any questions after. So please respect that."

She then read the statement:

"Good afternoon. Our families are once again asking for the public's help. It has been over seven weeks since Laci and the baby were taken from us."

Her voice broke and she struggled to contain herself as she continued with the statement.

"With her due date being this month, we feel it is critical to continue our efforts in looking for Laci everywhere we can," she said. "Every day we post and deliver fliers. We meet people who are not aware that she is missing. We cannot ignore that Laci's pregnancy may have had something to do with her abduction. After seven weeks she could be anywhere. So please do not think that you live too far from the situation to help."

She asked the public to log onto the Laci Peterson

Web site being run by a friend of Laci's family and print out missing persons fliers. "Please deliver them to your highway patrol, police and fire stations as well as any hospitals, clinics and pediatric offices," she said. "Post them at rest stops and hotels as you travel and any other high-traffic areas."

She thanked the Modesto Police Department "for continuing their efforts as they follow up on the tips as they come in."

"Unfortunately," she said. "There are no new developments." She asked people, again, to call the Laci Peterson tip line—she gave out the number—or their local police department. She said, "Your tip could be the one to bring her home."

She concluded on a spiritual note. "Paul the Apostle encouraged his brothers to not grow weary in doing good," she said. "Your prayers and encouragement have kept us from growing weary as we look for Laci. We thank you for your goodness in helping us."

She made no mention of Scott, of the controversy swirling around the affair, of the rift between the families. As the family stood to walk out of the press conference, reporters hit them with questions, which they tried to ignore.

"Thank you all very much," said Susan. "We're not going to comment."

Then a reporter asked about Scott not joining the rest of the family at the press conference, saying his absence raised more questions than answers.

"Could you just address that real quickly?" the reporter asked.

Scott's mother could not let it go.

"Scott is looking for Laci," she said. "That is the whole purpose and he has continued to do that from day one."

His sister added, with a coldness in her voice missing from the press conference, "He's in Modesto. He's 350 miles away. And we're here in San Diego. So we do what we can to help."

Scott would need all the help his family could provide.

Police had another warrant to search his house.

CHAPTER 13

Why the police had to conduct another search now, nearly two months after Laci disappeared, and following one other search, wasn't disclosed. Police released a statement saying only that "discoveries" during the investigation necessitated the search. Search warrant affidavits and other documents that spell out the reasons for searches had been filed under seal since the beginning. Despite numerous pleas before the judge by media lawyers, access was routinely denied in the name of justice.

The police arrived at 8 a.m. on Tuesday, February 18, five days after his family's press conference. Scott had just left the house and was driving his new 2002 Dodge pickup—the one he got by trading in Laci's Land Rover—down the street when he was stopped by police. He made a U-turn and found the cops waiting for him, warrant in hand. Over the next two days, an army of crime-scene investigators from the Modesto Police

Department, the Stanislaus County District Attorney's Office, even the Turlock Police Department from the neighboring town went through the little house and proceeded to clean the place out.

Bags upon bags of stuff—plastic bags, brown lunch bags, grocery bags—were hauled off by the rubber-glove-wearing CSI people, so many bags that reporters began to lose count: about four dozen the first day, maybe another dozen the next.

Scott's new Dodge pickup also got taken off the first morning, and now he was, again, without wheels. He disappeared for a while, then came back in a rented Chevy Tahoe. He helped police locate items from the search warrant list inside the house. But he wouldn't be staying for long. After talking to detectives in his driveway for about an hour, Scott threw up his arms, trudged into his back yard with investigators, then emerged from the house carrying two duffel bags and a clear plastic bag containing clothing. He had been evicted from his own home.

He got into the rental truck and took off while police continued to take out evidence in bags. He returned at least twice, one time to drop off food for his two cats, Siam and Gracie, another time to show the investigators a calendar datebook.

During one of the times Scott was away, Laci's sister Amy was summoned to the house by police to help find items.

The case by now truly was the circus that Laci's father-in-law had described. News trucks were parked up and down the street, their satellite towers reaching high into the sky. News helicopters roared overhead. The search was captured by TV cameras and aired live. People descended on the block to get front-row seats. It generated so much local interest that the little dead-end block, already something of a tourist attraction, was now seeing a constant stream of cars full of curious onlookers. Police finally erected barricades at either end of the street.

At one point on the first day, a befuddled UPS man tried to deliver a package from Laci's wine-of-the-month club, but police sent him—and the wine—back to his truck.

At 6 p.m., police wrapped up the search for the day and sealed off the property with crime-scene tape.

They returned the next day. The street was again blocked off, and for the rest of the day, police took measurements outside of the house and the driveway while technicians continued to tote out bags of evidence. Later it would be revealed that police also had warrants to search Scott's workplace and his "person," probably to retrieve hair or blood or both.

At the end of two more days of searches by police, it wasn't any clearer whether Scott was a wanted man or not. It wasn't known what was taken. It wasn't known what was going to happen next. All anybody knew was that Scott was locked in legal limbo.

"Scott Peterson is not a suspect yet," said police spokesman Doug Ridenour, "but he has not been cleared from this case."

Still, something in the investigation had changed, profoundly. What, police again wouldn't say. It could have been a major discovery from the search or a damning revelation during one of Scott's wiretapped phone calls. Maybe an important result came back from the crime lab. Or maybe investigators were simply admitting, officially, what common sense had been saying for a long time.

Either way, on Wednesday, March 5, two weeks after the latest search of Scott's house, Detective Craig Grogan, the lead investigator, who remained in the background while Ridenour and Chief Wasden did all the talking, called a press conference.

"As the investigation has progressed we have increasingly come to believe that Laci Peterson is the victim of a violent crime," said Grogan. "This investigation began as a missing persons case and we all were hopeful that Laci would return home safely. However, we have come to consider this a homicide case."

Later that day, Kim Petersen read a statement from Laci's family:

> "While this is a difficult day for the family, the police department and all of us, it is a necessary step because we do need to find Laci.
>
> "Since Laci first disappeared on December 24, our first priority has been to find her. It has been our priority every day since. Our family desperately needs to know where she is. We realize with every day that passes, the possibility of finding her alive diminishes.
>
> "Our lives in the last two and a half months have been horrific. It's been a never-ending nightmare. . . . We know someone out there has the information that can end our nightmare. We plead with them to tell us

where she is. We will continue our search for her. We will never stop looking for Laci. Until we find Laci, our lives are in turmoil. We feel we can't look on beyond today."

With that, Petersen said the Carole Sund-Carrington Memorial Reward Foundation announced a new reward—not for information aiding in Laci Peterson's safe return, but for information leading to the recovery of Laci Peterson's body.

In San Diego, Scott's mother, Jackie Peterson, said: "I would hope that if I were missing for a month or two, people wouldn't stop looking for me."

The search for Laci didn't in fact stop. Authorities became convinced they were wasting their time looking in the streams, rivers, canals and reservoirs in the Central Valley.

They now focused their search on a single body of water.

They were led there by evidence seized from Scott's house.

CHAPTER 14

Early in the case, a profiler from the U.S. Department of Justice had offered assistance to the Modesto Police Department. Among the profiler's contributions was a suggestion of where a person would dispose of a body, if that person happened to have committed a murder in the Modesto area. It was probably a deep body of water—a lake or reservoir—at a place that was easily accessible, such as a bridge.

It was for this reason that authorities searched as long as they did—three days—in the waters under the bridge that crosses Tulloch Reservoir northwest of Modesto. The water is deep—so deep one of the divers broke an eardrum—and accessible from the bridge. It's also why they searched, without drawing much attention, the New Melones Reservoir, where the water is more than 300 feet deep under one of the bridges. In this case, authorities used the same side-scan sonar that was employed in the San Francisco Bay search that turned up the anchor. Other reservoirs searched with sonar were the Don Pedro Reservoir to the west and the San Luis Reservoir to the south.

But by late January, police had received the results of an analysis of Scott's computer, which was taken from his home by search warrant on December 26 and 27. On it, they found downloaded nautical charts and tidal information for the San Francisco Bay. Also, police found paint marks on Scott's aluminum boat that looked similar to paint on the buoys in the bay waters off Berkeley Marina.

From the very beginning of the investigation, Scott had said he'd gone fishing there the day Laci had disappeared—he'd even provided the boat launch receipt— so this evidence was not in and of itself incriminating. Still, authorities looking for a watery grave for Laci could not rule out the possibility that Scott had been scoping out the bay. The only question was whether he was dumb enough to have dumped the body in exactly the place he'd told people he'd been.

As the searches of the reservoirs and waterways turned up nothing, authorities were increasingly convinced that he was that dumb.

In the second week of March, a week after declaring that the Laci Peterson case was now a homicide investigation, authorities from the Modesto Police Department and the Tuolumne County Sheriff's Department were back on the waters of the San Francisco Bay, this time using sonar to search off of Richmond Point, north of the Berkeley Marina. They were working with a private firm, Ralston & Associates of Idaho, who had provided sonar services during the searches of some of the reservoirs and had worked with law-enforcement agencies throughout the West on criminal cases and drownings.

Searchers were now off Richmond Point because among the charts found on Scott's computer was one for a shipping lane in this area, where the water was considerably deeper than other areas to accommodate the tankers and cargo ships. Deeper water also would be a better place to dump a weighted body.

On Wednesday, March 12, while scanning the bottom of the bay in about 40-foot waters, Gene Ralston saw something interesting pop up on his shipboard computer screen. It went by too fast to get a good look. But that night he reviewed the images on his computer and saw something that could have been a body. On the screen, it was only a small image, and there were no limbs that he could make out. Just something sort of oval-shaped that didn't appear to be a rock or log—or anchor. A closer inspection was needed. The next day, searchers went back to the location. The wind was blowing strong and the waves were washing over their boat. One wave was so huge, it knocked a duffel bag full of equipment into the bay.

From this precarious perch, searchers sent down a camera.

Ralston was shocked.

To his eyes, the scene on the video monitor looked like a body, face down, with what appeared to be tattered clothing undulating like streamers. The body was covered in crabs.

There was no VCR hooked to the monitor and an attempt to videotape the screen with another camera created an unusable picture. So there was no good record of what the men on the boat saw. Then the search had to be called off early. The water was so rough that the searchers had to head for shore. Rain was in the forecast for the next five days straight.

When they returned two weeks later, on March 29, whatever they had seen in the shipping lane was gone.

There would be great disagreement later over whether this was a body—to say nothing of whether it was the body of Laci Peterson. Ralston would speculate that it was; Modesto police would say it wasn't.

Either way, the debate would become moot.

In just two weeks, there would be no more reason to continue the search for Laci Peterson.

CHAPTER 15

It's 21 acres of canine heaven: grassy expanses, rocks and trees, and no leashes required. From the western peak of Point Isabel, jutting into the San Francisco Bay just north of Berkeley, and along the bayside trail to the canal bridge to the north, dogs can run free in the cool bay breezes, chasing tennis balls and sloshing in the salt water. "A wonderful place for nature, dogs and dog lovers!" reads the full-color brochure from a group called PIDO—Point Isabel Dog Owners and Friends. In the group's logo, a happy pooch pokes his head out of the "O" in PIDO. Along the trail, there are faucets with hoses to give dogs baths. More pampered pets can go to the Mudpuppy's Tub & Scrub, an onsite doggy day spa, that provides, according to the "menu of services," elevated tubs, warm water, shampoo, two towels, combs, brushes and a friendly helpful staff. A full-service treatment runs $15 for small dogs to $31 for large dogs, with such extras as an herbal flea dip for $5, a nail trim for

$3, a fur conditioner for $3 and a blow-dry for $5.

At the north end of the park, at a wooden bridge over a canal, the dogs will find a little less love—leashes are now required—but the environment is still friendly, with a mile-long path perfect for walking pooches through an unspoiled shoreline of marsh grass, tall reeds and tiny streams with a view of the Golden Gate Bridge due west, the sounds of the lapping bay water and wind through the reeds almost drowning out the roar of traffic from Interstate 580 a few hundred yards to the east and the occasional toot from a freight train. Reality hits when the wetlands end about a mile north of Point Isabel, and the trail now runs alongside an industrial park and condominiums before making its way into Richmond Marina Bay.

The days leading up to the weekend of Saturday, April 12, were not good ones for dog-walking. A cold rain pummeled the Bay Area and the winds were fierce, slamming into the park from the west. Waves crashed against the boulders on the shoreline, sending foamy spray up to the grass. But then that Sunday afternoon, the stormy weather subsided, and the dogs and their human companions were out once again along the San Francisco Bay Trail.

It was at the northern end of the trail, just after the wetlands meet industry, where two people walking their dog spotted a small light-colored object lying in the marshy mud about fifteen feet away from the water. This was an area normally covered by water, but on this afternoon the tide was out and the marsh was exposed.

It was the body of a tiny baby.

The next morning, Monday, April 14, about a mile to the south in the Point Isabel Regional Shoreline Park, another dog was being taken for a walk. As the woman followed her dog, she saw something light-colored lodged in the rocks a few feet from the water. She got a closer look, and then, at 11:43 a.m., dialed 911.

It was the torso of a body—with no arms, feet or head—lying with its back up.

Two bodies in two days, one a baby, the other appearing to be an adult, each being found by dog-walkers within about a mile of each other on the Richmond shoreline, after a nasty weekend storm.

A call was placed by park police to the Modesto Police Department.

Police Chief Roy Wasden's pager went off while he was eating at a Mexican restaurant in town. The message was to call the assistant chief.

Now.

When Wasden heard about the discoveries of the bodies from the park police, his first thought was, At last, the break we've been waiting for. Thousands of hours spent searching every body of water from the Sierra foothills to the San Francisco Bay, and finally the discovery. It was also something of a relief. He knew now the department had not jumped the gun in declaring the Laci Peterson case a homicide investigation.

His next thought: Where was Scott Peterson?

Scott hadn't been seen in weeks. There had been no

surveillance placed on him. Police had to find out where he was, immediately, and put a tail on him. He had business connections in Mexico, had possibly even traveled there recently. It was imperative that, having come this far, police did not let Scott Peterson slip away.

Within 24 hours, four agents from the state Department of Justice were following Scott. A satellite tracking device was affixed to his car. A judge approved another round of phone taps.

Wasden got his people to the scene as quickly as possible. A helicopter ferried investigators to the bay, delivering them to a parking lot at the park. Others drove. Through the course of the day and into the night some twenty investigators would arrive, including members of the Stanislaus County District Attorney's Office.

Also called shortly after the body was found was Kim Petersen, spokeswoman and advisor for Laci's family. She drove to the home of Sharon Rocha and Ron Grantski and gave them the news: The body of an adult and a baby had been found on the shore of San Francisco Bay just north of the Berkeley Marina. Neither had been identified. But Modesto police had arrived in force.

Sharon wept. They tried to think positively. Maybe it was another false alarm. They'd had more than their share since Laci disappeared—the body that had turned out to be an anchor, the sighting at the grocery store that wasn't true. Sharon asked to be apprised of all the developments.

There was no such special treatment for the family of Scott Peterson. His mother had to find out about the discovery of the bodies from news reports in the afternoon. She called Modesto police, who had little information beyond what was on the news. Their investigators still hadn't arrived at the scene. Jackie Peterson called her son.

Then she prayed that the body wasn't Laci's.

As crime-scene technicians worked the scene, officials in Modesto tried to play it conservatively. They said the adult could be a drowning victim, could be anybody. The baby's body may have nothing to do with the adult. Doug Ridenour told a news conference: "At this point, we have no information, nor has the recovered body been identified as that of Laci Peterson. Until such time as our department has been notified and it has been confirmed that the East Bay body is related to the Modesto case, this is an East Bay Regional Park District Police Department case." Added Modesto Police Sergeant Ron Cloward, who had headed the search, "All it is at this point is that they had a body wash up. We have no indication at this point that it has anything to do with Laci."

The team of investigators worked the scene until 2 a.m. Tuesday morning.

Common sense would dictate that if these weren't the bodies of Laci and Conner, found as they were, where they were, so close to where Scott had gone fishing, this would be a breathtaking coincidence. But in reality, authorities didn't know very much.

The bodies were taken from the shoreline, bagged and placed in white coroner's vans and driven to the Contra

Costa County coroner's office in Martinez, 10 miles away. Perhaps the coroner could find some answers as to how these people had died and how they'd ended up on the shore.

The early speculation was that the weekend's storms had churned the waters and dislodged the bodies from whatever was holding them underwater. If the bodies had been in the shipping channel, a passing tanker could have whipped up the water enough to free them. Another possibility was a chemical change in the bodies that made them more buoyant. Bacteria flourish in a submerged body when spring arrives and the surrounding water reaches temperatures of more than 40 degrees. The bacteria emit a gas that can cause a body to float.

Either way, it was clear that the adult had been in the water for some time. An expert would be called in to narrow down a time period, but from the level of decomposition to the adult, the body easily could have been underwater for several months.

There was no identification on the adult body. Indeed, there was very little left of the body, mostly just skeleton, a little skin. The coroner could tell it was a woman with a petite build. She had taken a pounding, either before or after death, as many of her ribs were fractured.

The coroner could not identify her with the fastest, easiest method—dental records—since the body was missing the head. In fact, the body was missing the first six vertebrae, from the neck to the upper back. The body also was missing both hands and forearms; only the arms from the shoulder to the elbow remained. Both feet were missing. The left leg was missing from the hip down, with both the shinbone and thighbone gone.

It wasn't clear how the body had come to lose the head and limbs, but the coroner found no evidence of "tool marks"—the little scuffs and nicks and gouges that are left by saws, knives, hatchets or other implements of violence. With extensive evidence of "animal feeding," as well as decomposition and normal battering by the tides, the body may have simply started to fall apart, starting with the head, hands, feet and some limbs, the coroner believed.

These factors also may have accounted for the ravage to the stomach area. Most of the woman's organs, including her heart, liver, spleen, lungs and intestines, were gone, leaving the cavity empty.

The coroner could tell that this had been a woman carrying a child. There was an opening near the top of the uterus and the cervix was closed. This meant the baby did not leave the mother's body through the birth canal—otherwise the cervix would have been open—but through that hole in the uterus.

As for cause of death, the coroner could only say this: Undetermined.

In examining the baby's body, what stood out immediately was how well-preserved it was compared to that of the woman's body. The baby was in such good condition that the coroner could tell, for instance, that it was a boy. All limbs and extremities were intact, as was the head. The baby did have a deep cut on his chest and right shoulder. Although the cause of the gash couldn't be determined, it appeared similar to the sort of injury commonly seen among bodies taken from water: the mark from a boat propeller.

The age of the baby also couldn't be determined with pinpoint accuracy. All the coroner would say was that the boy appeared to be a "full-term" baby, which would be about the age of Laci's child. At the time of her disappearance it was believed she was eight months pregnant, though due dates are always estimates. Even the use of a sonogram—which Scott and Laci had had taken of Conner that previous September—is not exact.

The coroner did note, however, that there was no placenta and no umbilical cord. This, combined with the baby's age and the different states of decomposition of the child and woman's bodies, raised the provocative question of whether the baby was born alive before the mother was killed, or whether the boy had left his mother well after death.

If the dead woman was in fact the baby's mother, then there was evidence the child did separate from mother long after death. If the mother's body was face down, it could have shielded the baby from the watery elements. The baby then could have been separated from the mother as she rose to the surface through the opening in the uterus and out the decomposed stomach area.

There was another factor, however, that raised questions about this grisly theory. Adhesive tape was wrapped around the baby's neck, knotted with an inch of space from the neck. The tape then trailed under the baby's left arm and over the chest. How the tape got there wasn't clear. It could simply have been garbage floating around in the bay that somehow got over the baby's head as it floated toward shore.

The more eerie possibility was that a person had wrapped and knotted the tape around the baby's head.

This opened a whole can of theoretical worms. To do this, the baby would obviously have to have already left the mother's body, either alive or dead.

Could the baby have been born alive, then killed later and tossed in the bay?

Was the mother alive when the baby was born?

When exactly did they die?

And how?

And what monster could have done this?

Authorities not only didn't have answers to these questions, they didn't have positive identifications. To determine the identity of the woman and the parentage of the baby, tissue and bone samples were sent to the state crime lab for DNA testing, which could take weeks to complete, if it could be done at all. There were questions of whether the woman's body was in good enough condition to yield DNA suitable for testing.

Thus would begin a grueling waiting game.

Modesto police officials huddled with authorities from the prosecutor's office to go over how to proceed. There were by now a number of jurisdictions involved, from the Bay Area authorities, to the state investigators and crime lab specialists, to police in the San Diego area where Scott's family lived. Coordination was essential.

Laci's family, meanwhile, could only sit and wait. They weren't giving interviews. But on the day after the woman's body was found, family spokeswoman Kim Petersen called a press conference to read a message from the family:

"Obviously this is a very difficult time for our family as we await the results of the DNA testing. These past 3½ months have been a constant nightmare for us. From the beginning, we have done all we can to find Laci and will continue to do so until she's found.

"This waiting is the worst. While in the news reports these are two bodies that have been found, to us they could potentially be our daughter and grandson, our sister and nephew, loving members of our family, or possibly someone else's family who is experiencing our same pain. Please be considerate of that fact.

"We believe that if this is Laci, God has allowed her to be found because our family needs to know where she is and what has happened to her. If this turns out to be Laci, we want the animal responsible for this heinous act to pay. We will do all we can to pursue justice for Laci and Conner.

"We ask for your thoughts and prayers as we wait. We would like to thank all the people who have been so supportive of us during these past months. Your prayers, hugs, cards and e-mails mean more than you know. We don't know how we would have made it through each day without all of you.

"During this time of waiting, we ask that you respect our privacy and our need to be together as a family. We will not be conducting any interviews prior to the test results.

"Thank you.

"Laci's family."

The task of identifying the remains was assigned to the DNA program at the state crime lab in Richmond, the bayside city where the bodies were found. Normally, authorities prefer to use the faster and cheaper dental record comparisons or fingerprint checks to identify bodies. But in many cases, particularly children, who don't have dental records, or in cases in which the body's fingers are missing or badly decomposed, DNA testing is the only alternative available. Bankrolled by a $2 fee on death certificates, the lab was born out of the efforts of a state senator named Jackie Speier who was shocked to find out how many bodies remained without positive IDs—some 1,800 adults and 200 children. Now the lab had two more.

On Wednesday, April 16, John Tonkyn, supervisor of the missing person DNA program, said testing focused only on whether the remains were those of Laci and her baby and "we don't have another person in mind." The only question was whether the badly decomposed remains would yield enough usable DNA to test. The plan was to compare the DNA samples from the two bodies to see if they were related, and then to compare the woman's DNA against genetic material extracted from a strand of Laci's hair in a brush at her home and from the DNA from the inner-cheek cells swabbed from the mouths of Laci's mother and father. They also planned to compare the baby's DNA against the genetic material in a blood sample from Scott, obtained by a search warrant.

By late Wednesday evening, there was positive news. Screening tests on samples from the baby's muscle tissue and from his femur, or thighbone, found that there was in fact good enough quality DNA for testing.

The woman's body, which was in worse shape, offered a greater challenge. Technicians extracted DNA from the woman's tibia, or shinbone, and from muscle tissue, and hoped it was in good enough condition. As the testing continued, Stanislaus County District Attorney Jim Brazelton said out loud what everybody had already been thinking. "I feel pretty strong it is [Laci]," he told *The Modesto Bee*. "It's too much of a coincidence to have a female and a baby found close to each other a day apart and no others were reported missing. If I were a betting man, I'd put money on it."

Again, there would be good news from the lab. The woman's tibia produced viable DNA. Technicians now had enough genetic material from both the baby and the woman to test. They opted for PCR testing—short for polymerase chain reaction—which allowed for technicians to test very small samples of DNA, which was the case here. PCR works like genetic Xeroxing—a small sample of DNA is copied, or replicated, into a larger version, which is chopped up into segments and sorted, with the results printed out in a bar code. These results would then be compared to the known samples from Laci and her parents, as well as against a control sample.

The additional benefit of this method of testing was that it could be done quickly. The results were expected within two days—by Friday, April 18.

Good Friday.

By now, Modesto police and the district attorney's office were acting under the assumption that it was a foregone conclusion the tests would prove to be the bodies of Laci and Conner. And so, on Thursday, Modesto Detective Craig Grogan, the lead investigator in the case, and Detective Phil Owen—both just back from the Bay

Area—joined with Stanislaus County prosecutors for a secret meeting with Superior Court Judge Wray Ladine in his chambers. People saw them go in, then come out about a half-hour later, grim-faced and offering no comment.

Then, Grogan and three other lawmen—detectives Jon Buehler and Al Brocchini and their sergeant, Al Carter—got into two unmarked police cars and headed for San Diego. They arrived just after midnight, early on the morning of Good Friday.

They were carrying a document signed by Ladine. It was addressed to The People of the State of California:

To any peace officer of said state:

Complaint upon oath having been this day made before me by Detective Craig Grogan, I find that there is probable cause to believe that two counts of the crime of 187 PC, homicide, committed on or about Monday December 23, 2002, or Tuesday December 24, 2002, in the county of Stanislaus by Scott Lee Peterson, date of birth 10/24/72.

You are therefore commanded forthwith to arrest the above-named defendant and bring him/her before any magistrate in Stanislaus County pursuant to Penal Code Section 187.

The within named defendant may be admitted to bail in the sum of: No Bail.

It was signed by the judge and included details of Scott, including the name of his employer—Tradecorp—his address and a physical description: 6-foot, 200 pounds with brown hair and brown eyes.

It was time to get Scott Peterson.

CHAPTER 16

The script was written. The scene was set. The action was to go down at a spectacular location, the Torrey Pines Golf Course, with fairways perched on tall bluffs that overlook the Pacific coastline of San Diego County. There had been a dramatic build-up: taunts and hard feelings on both sides.

Would the man from San Diego prevail or fall? An anxious public wanted to know.

It was the final round of the 2003 Buick Invitational, and the hometown boy, Phil Mickelson, was locked in a do-or-die battle with superstar Tiger Woods. Mickelson was just two strokes behind Woods and had not only the home-course advantage, but history on his side. He had won twice at Torrey Pines, in 2001 and 2000. Woods had won once in 1999. It was a true rivalry, intensified this year by Mickelson making disparaging comments about Woods' equipment—the golf equivalent of trash-talking.

On Sunday, February 16, the last day of the tournament, fans packed the course, standing shoulder to shoulder down the entire length of the first fairway, to see who would win this heavily hyped showdown.

Tiger got on a roll, shooting a four-under par 68, and ended up taking home $810,000 and the thirty-fifth PGA victory of his career. Mickelson came out flat, shooting a par 72 to finish the tournament tied for fourth place. He told reporters later, "I wasn't really there much."

How much of any of this was followed by Mickelson's onetime teammate on his high school golf squad isn't known. Scott Peterson had other things on his mind in February 2003. Two days after the tournament, his house was searched by members of the Modesto Police Department as part of what was then still being called a missing persons case.

Scott Peterson had played with Phil Mickelson during Scott's freshman year at University of San Diego High School. When Mickelson left high school on his way to golfing glory, young Scott had taken his place as team leader. Years later, Scott's coach, Dave Thoennes, would say nice things about Scott, describing him as a great leader and a great golfer: dependable, focused, confident and friendly. He was named the most valuable player for two years, and made *The San Diego Union-Tribune*'s All-Academic Team three years. Some of Scott's teammates wouldn't be so kind, describing him as an arrogant loner who was tolerated only because he was so good with a club.

Whatever people may have thought of him as a player

or a person, Scott's golfing career would peter out shortly after high school. He got the partial scholarship to play golf at Arizona State University, then left shortly thereafter for junior college and Cal Poly, San Luis Obispo, marriage, and a career selling fertilizer. Although he would continue to play golf for fun and relaxation, the closest Scott would ever get to sharing time on the links with old teammate Mickelson was watching him on TV dueling with the likes of Tiger Woods.

On the morning of Friday, April 18, Scott Peterson was driving around San Diego County in a purple Mercedes-Benz. He hadn't been in Modesto for weeks and the folks who knew him would be surprised at his appearance. It didn't match the description on the warrant. His brown hair was dyed a curious shade of reddish blond and he had grown a goatee with a matching dye job.

He was being followed this morning, as he had been throughout the week, by agents from the state Department of Justice. It must not have been the most discreet of tail jobs, because Scott would periodically taunt his followers. While driving around to the homes of friends and family members, he would make hand gestures at the agents. At one point, he pulled over, got out of the car and yelled, "Why don't you go ahead and arrest me?"

Around 11 a.m., Scott's Mercedes was driving in the direction of the Torrey Pines Golf Course. It was a holiday, but golfers were turning out anyway to play a round at the picturesque course, where golfers can pay up to $195 in greens fees. Employees at the driving range showed up for work as usual, but knew that something was different. Two men wearing what looked like bulletproof vests over street clothes were standing around with guns in their hands. The employees didn't worry too much; a lot of celebrities play the course and these men might be bodyguards.

Ten minutes later, at 11:10 a.m., Scott's Mercedes approached the intersection of Callen and Torrey Pines roads. Scott was waving at the agents who were following him.

Although the DNA test results on the bodies found by the San Francisco Bay were not in yet, the agents carried a secured probable-cause arrest warrant—one that allows an arrest before the filing of criminal charges as long as authorities convince a judge of the validity of their reasons for that arrest. The officers—Department of Justice Special Agent Supervisor Ernie Limon, Special Agent Peter Shear and CHP Officer Claude Jubran—pulled over Scott.

He was arrested without incident in a parking lot. He was wearing a blue sweater, white polo shirt, white shorts and Nike tennis shoes and was not carrying a gun. He was handcuffed and turned over to the four Modesto police detectives who had arrived in San Diego the night before.

Another showdown at Torrey Pines fizzled in the final round.

The boy from San Diego put up no fight in the end.

Authorities had been concerned that Scott might run away to Mexico. The border was less than thirty miles away. When they arrested him, they found what they considered proof that their fears were warranted. In addition to the new blond look, Scott was carrying his brother's ID and $10,000 in cash.

Three hours later, at 2 p.m., police in Modesto released this terse bulletin to the media: "There has been a significant change in the Laci Peterson investigation." The memo said a press conference would be held that evening to explain, though by now word of Scott Peterson's arrest was all over the news. The only question was whether authorities had the DNA test results back.

The answer would be given first to Laci's family. Police Chief Roy Wasden, in full uniform, a black ribbon over his badge, walked up to the front door of the home of Laci's mother and stepfather. With him was Police Captain Greg Savelli, wearing a dark suit appropriate for a funeral.

They emerged shortly thereafter, and prepared for the news conference.

It would be a frantic evening. Attorney General Lockyer had just gotten married to Nadia Maria Davis in a ceremony in the East Bay when he got the word from the state crime lab. Lockyer ducked out of his own wedding reception and headed for the lab in nearby Richmond to hold a news conference at 6 p.m.

It was carried live, nationally, by cable television.

"There is no question in our minds," Lockyer announced, "that the unidentified female is Laci Peterson and the unidentified fetus is the biological child of Laci and Scott Peterson." He added: "We are scientifically convinced that the match is one in billions."

It was official. Laci Peterson, who'd disappeared as she was preparing to walk her dog, was found by a dog-walker.

In a CNN interview with Larry King, Lockyer would then make the now-infamous remark: "This is a compellingly strong case . . . I would call the odds slam-dunk that he is going to be convicted."

Scott was arrested even before the test results came in, out of fear that he would flee, he said.

"We started to worry," the attorney general added. "He was aware of the surveillance teams, was waving at them and being, you know, kind of a smart-aleck, and so they finally decided that they ought to just pull him in."

Ninety miles away, in Modesto, Police Chief Wasden held his own news conference.

"It's been truly a difficult four months, not just for our community, but for our nation," he said. "This is a tragedy that is affecting many lives." Among them were the lives of Scott's parents, Lee and Jackie Peterson, Wasden said. "And they'll have to deal with that. They wanted to believe in their son, and they chose to do that. We went through with our investigation." Laci's family, he said, was "devastated" when told the news.

Wasden said that as the investigation unfolded, "It became clear that it was important to keep track of Scott." Nothing else seemed to make more sense. They had posted a huge reward, scoured the Central Valley and the Bay Area, enjoyed the benefit of saturation news coverage, all in vain. "Had anyone known where she was, we would have heard about it," the chief said, which is why he'd reluctantly declared the case a homicide investigation, even as he hoped he was wrong. "I would have loved to have egg on my face," he said.

So while police "prayed for a different outcome," he said, the more investigators knew, the more things changed behind the scenes, the only logical course of action was clear: arrest Scott Peterson in the murders of his wife and unborn son. Wasden again refused to say why. Pressed by reporters on the reason for Scott's arrest, the chief refused to get into the evidence, but made it clear it didn't hinge on the identities of the bodies.

"I'm not going to get into motive," he said. "We [decided to] make our arrest before we had the DNA results."

Afterwards District Attorney Jim Brazelton announced that Peterson would be charged with two counts of murder; one of the victims was killed before he was even born. This would raise controversial legal and moral issues in the coming weeks.

It also meant that this was a capital case—a fate Scott could have avoided three months earlier had he struck the deal to tell police where Laci's body was.

Now, there was no talk of a deal.

Or bail.

"Bail?" asked Brazelton. "Why?"

After the visit by Chief Wasden and the police captain, Laci's family didn't leave the house and didn't speak to reporters. Throughout the evening, people were seen bringing in food and cards. At one point, the police chaplain was seen going into the house.

Instead, family spokeswoman Kim Peterson read a statement:

"Just as Christmas Eve is a family time, Easter is also a time for families. We request that you allow our family to have time this weekend to deal with these recent developments together in private. We ask for your understanding during this time and respect our need for this privacy. Please do not call any family members at their homes or on their cell phones. The family will make a statement Monday afternoon. We appreciate those of you who honor our request. Please place all media requests through me and understand that hundreds of calls are coming in. All requests will be documented. Thank you for your support during this very difficult time."

Petersen would give no more details of how the family was coping, except to say this: "Families in these circumstances will always tell you that not knowing is the worst part. They have answers. They don't have to worry every single minute of every single day about where Laci is."

Scott's lawyer, Kirk McAllister, issued a defiant no comment. A sign on his front window said, "No Media." At the San Diego home of Scott Peterson's parents, there was no police chief visit, no badges with ribbons over them, no chaplain—just seven TV trucks and two dozen reporters milling around on the sidewalk. A sign posted on the front of their home read: "We will not talk to you at our house." But a Copley News Service reporter was able to catch up with Jackie Peterson while she was walking her springer spaniel. In what was called a "brief" interview, she said of her son, "He misses his wife . . . This is the worst thing that's ever happened to us. It will probably never end."

CHAPTER 17

Before there was a Modesto Police Department, there were the Regulators.

They were black-masked vigilantes who in the late 1800s would periodically ransack the brothels, gambling houses, dance halls and opium dens, then leave notes saying things like: "You are hereby notified to leave Modesto within twenty-four hours and never return, under peril of your lives." Nobody knew for certain who the men behind the masks were, but it's widely believed they were the town's normally upstanding businessmen and farmers.

The Regulators would put their masks away and go back to their shops and fields once the new marshal took over and rid the city of the likes of Barney Garner, the saloonkeeper whose political career ended in blood.

But late one night a century later the spirit of the Regulators, of Modesto's past, again haunted the streets paved by the railroads.

• • •

"Murderer!"

"Burn in hell!"

"Confess and repent!"

"Hang him!"

The words were shouted and emblazoned on signs. In the hours leading up to midnight, a crowd of about 200 people had formed outside the Stanislaus County Jail. They were awaiting the arrival of Modesto's most famous villain since Barney Garner. Many in this crowd had felt for Scott, prayed for Scott, searched the streets and streams and fields of Modesto for Scott, even donated money for Scott, only to have it all come to this.

Although anger rippled through the crowd, it would be an overstatement to call it an unruly mob out for blood. This wasn't nineteenth century Modesto. And the TV cameras were there, as were the police, in force.

Police had blocked off 12th Street between H and I Streets to make a clear lane for the two unmarked cars carrying four detectives and the man who had been arrested about 11 hours earlier.

Those who weren't calling for Scott Peterson's head were making a party out of the event. Some in the crowd brought cameras to catch the momentous occasion. They jostled with photographers, TV crews and reporters to get the best possible view. Others brought children. One father lifted his baby and told a TV crew he was doing this "to show Scott what he missed out on."

As the cars drove up, many could clearly see Peterson in the back seat. He hardly looked evil—just tired, head down. He looked like a guy who had spent too much time in the sun on the golf course: bleached hair, white polo shirt, tan shorts.

His arms were placed behind him, his wrists cuffed. He had been like that the entire way up from San Diego. Sitting next to him was the lead investigator in the case, Detective Craig Grogan. Neither acknowledged the crowd.

When the cars drove up, the crowd burst into cheers and applause.

Scott was led into the building for booking. He could clearly be seen through the slats of a window going through the booking process, handing over his belt and shoes to deputies. He was fingerprinted and photographed. He took off his khaki shorts and polo shirt and was issued a red jail jumpsuit—red for maximum security. He was permitted a single phone call. He spoke to an old friend in Ventura County; what they talked about, nobody knew. Jailers then led him to his cell.

The next day, Saturday, April 19, Scott awoke, not in a three-bedroom two-bath home with a pool and newly remodeled kitchen on Covena Avenue, but in a 6-foot-by-9-foot cell with a stainless-steel toilet. He had spent a short night on a two-inch mattress, incarcerated on a murder warrant without bail. He was described by a sheriff's spokesman as anxious, courteous and quiet—typical of a first-timer in the jail. At one point he told his jailers, "Your staff has been very professional and fair. Thank you." Some of his new neighbors weren't so nice. Scott was heckled and harassed by other inmates, though no altercations broke out.

The house he used to live in was now a shrine to Laci, the front yard a garden of cut flowers, stuffed animals, candles and cards, the sidewalk lined with people in tears. Mourners kneeled on the lawn and prayed. Children sobbed. A homemade cross on the grass read: "We prayed every day that Laci and baby Conner would come home. Now, Laci and baby Conner are home with the Lord." A message of a different sort was posted on a sign on a tree at the house: "Attention Scott: God knows and we know you did it. Just give yourself up!"

In jail, special precautions were taken to protect him from other inmates—and himself. He had his own cell and was watched constantly by a sheriff's deputy. There were worries about his mental health; he was offered a counselor, but refused. After a breakfast of a cheese omelet and milk, he made phone calls, had beef vegetable soup for lunch and chicken soup for dinner, then met with his lawyer, Kirk McAllister, in the evening. He asked for a haircut, but was told he would have to wait until the once-a-month barber arrived and get his hair cut at the same time as the rest of the jail population. Twice a week, he would be allowed to exercise for ninety minutes on the roof by walking around in shackles. He would be allowed five books and ten photographs. He would have access to a pay phone. But he didn't grant any jailhouse interviews, didn't take any visitors from the press. His talking days were over for now. McAllister refused to comment.

As had been the case from the very beginning, it was left to others to defend Scott in the court of public opinion. On Sunday, April 20—Easter Sunday—his parents, who had remained quiet on the day Scott was arrested, let it all out, providing a spirited defense of their jailed and accused son, and unleashing a blistering attack against the police and prosecution. It came in the form of an interview with *Time* magazine reporter Jill Underwood. Their words were so impassioned—and newsworthy—that the magazine didn't wait to publish them, instead running the interview on the *Time* Web site.

"We're grieving for the loss of Scott's wife and the baby. Our family is just devastated, and we feel an equal amount of pain for the Rocha family—Sharon and Ron and the whole family," Lee Peterson said. "But . . . our son is innocent. We know that. We've known it from day one."

"They know it too," added Jackie, referring to Laci's family. "They supported him fully until the police misled them, and that was to divide and separate him from them. He was their support. They were his support."

Lee said, "I would ask everyone to consider Scott's family. We're a good family. We don't have a record of anything."

"He doesn't either," said Jackie. "You can look."

"He doesn't," said Lee. "There was no domestic violence."

"No drugs. No financial problems," said Jackie. "He worked three jobs to put himself through college and put his wife through college. They both worked hard to get everything they had, and they were enjoying it to the hilt. And they adored each other."

"We were with them the week before Christmas, and you never saw a more loving couple," said Lee.

"Laci's mother stated the same thing prior to the police going to them," said Jackie. "All her family talked about how much they loved each other. How happy they were. How happily married people they were."

But the police, said Lee, saw fit to ignore the facts.

"We're just very critical of the way the Modesto police has handled this investigation," said Lee. "They worked strictly on a theory that was dreamt up by this lead detective within the first eight hours, and they've pursued it backward from there and they have neglected so many good leads."

Even before Scott had his first court appearance, his parents were alluding to what would become a defense theme: a rush-to-judgment by cops who ignored any evidence that tended to exonerate Scott.

"I think it's inappropriate for the police to be preening and patting themselves on the back for a good job of four months when they've done a cheap shot . . . is what they've performed," Jackie complained. "Not only that, but they were preening and patting themselves when the announcement of who those bodies were. That's totally inappropriate. If they want to pat themselves on the back, they should have a party somewhere else. I'm just appalled at that, that our public people are like that. You have a district attorney calling this a slam-dunk before there's even an arraignment. I'm feeling like I'm living in Nazi Germany or the Soviet Union. I'm just sick of this."

She began to cry.

"I think every man out there should be in fear if this is the way the police worked," she said. "If a crime happens to your wife, you'd better know you're with six people and they weren't drunk and they are good friends who are going to be able to put up with this. If they have any kind of shady character, the police will dismiss them and you'll be ruined."

More than 300 miles away, along the shores of the San Francisco Bay, people spent Easter Sunday playing with their dogs at Point Isabel, a return to normalcy save for one thing: another shrine, like the one at the Covena Avenue house, had been created on the grass near where Laci Peterson's body had been found. There were stuffed Easter bunnies, teddy bears, wilted flowers and soggy notes that said things like.

"To Laci and Conner, you are a fighter. Let us get answers from your death."

Then there was this one, its anger belying the Easter themes of redemption and forgiveness.

"Take your baby and go to the light, Laci," it read. "They caught the bastard."

CHAPTER 18

Rain fell on Modesto on the morning of Monday, April 21. Outside the Stanislaus County Courthouse, 11th Street was lined with television news trucks, their satellite dishes aimed skyward, the correspondents delivering their reports from under the protection of white canopies. At about 10 a.m., Scott Peterson's temporary government-provided lawyer, Public Defender Tim Bazar, visited him in jail. His father also met with him. Lee Peterson had lost none of his fire from the *Time* magazine interview of the day before. "My son is innocent, and it is going to come out," he told reporters as he left the jail. "I am confident of that."

Two of Scott's closest friends weren't so sure. Mike and Heather Richardson—the best man and maid of honor at his wedding, the couple who put him up in their house after the Amber revelation—expressed doubts about his innocence. "After the fact, his actions were strange. I don't know about suspicious, but strange,"

Heather said on NBC's *Today* show. The couple had spoken to Scott after his arrest and they said he sounded like he had been crying. They didn't talk about much, but they did bring up his new hair color. He told them the hair got bleached from swimming in a friend's pool.

Asked if they still supported him, Mike Richardson said, "You know, it's kind of hard to say. You know, we—They were both our best friends. And thinking that—that there's a chance Scott could have done this to Laci is just unfathomable. And, you know, I don't know what to think."

Security was tight for Scott's arraignment before Superior Court Judge Nancy Ashley. Seven bailiffs were summoned for security, rather than the usual two or three for a court session. There were only fifty-six seats in Ashley's courtroom, and it was the hottest media ticket since the O.J. trial. The availability for the press was reduced because seats were reserved for the general public and family members.

Lee and Jackie Peterson entered the courtroom first, followed by Sharon Rocha. All eyes were on the two women, one the mother of the victim, the other of the accused. Jackie approached Sharon. The women embraced.

"I'm so sorry. I'm so sorry," Jackie told Sharon.

They sat down on opposite sides of the courtroom.

The bailiff then led Scott into the courtroom. He wore the red jail jumpsuit with a white T-shirt visible underneath. His hands were shackled in front of him, with a chain around his waist. His ankles were also shackled.

He clinked as he walked. He still had the bristly bleached hair, trimmed shorter, and the goatee was gone.

He was led to his seat at the counsel table, right in front of where his parents were seated in the audience section.

"I'll call the case of *People* versus *Scott Lee Peterson*," said Judge Ashley. She then addressed Scott. "Mr. Peterson, is Scott Lee Peterson your true and correct name?"

"Yes, it is," said Scott.

"Is your birth date correctly listed as October 24, 1972?"

"Yes."

"And you, sir, are charged in Count I of the Complaint with a violation of Penalty Code Section 187—murder."

The judge continued: "There's a special allegation alleged that during the commission of that offense that you acted intentionally, deliberately and with premeditation. There's also an enhancement alleged entitled 'Termination of Pregnancy,' alleging that during the commission of that offense that you did personally inflict injury on Laci Denise Peterson and did terminate her pregnancy."

As Ashley spoke, Sharon Rocha began to cry. Her husband Ron Grantski pulled her close.

Scott's parents sat in stony silence.

"Count 2," the judge said, "is charging you with violation of Penal Code Section 187 alleging murder with that same special allegation—that during the commission of that offense that you acted intentionally, deliberately and with premeditation.

"There's also a special allegation alleged as to Counts

1 and 2 that those offenses were committed with one murder or more in the first or second degree, and it's a special circumstance within the meaning of Penal Code Section 190.2(a)(3)."

Translation: Scott qualified for the death penalty.

When she read him this, Scott shut his eyes and began to lose his composure. He then pulled himself back together.

Except for the judge's voice, the courtroom was silent.

"And, Mr. Peterson, are you in a situation where you can hire an attorney?" the judge asked.

"No," Scott said without elaboration.

"Mr. Bazar," the judge said to the public defender, "the public defender's office will be appointed to represent Mr. Peterson."

Turning back to Scott, the judge said, "Mr. Peterson, I'll ask you to enter pleas to Counts 1 and 2. What are your pleas to Counts 1 and 2?"

In a strong, clear voice, Scott answered, "I am not guilty."

"And do you deny or admit the special allegation in the enhancement that is alleged?" she asked, referring to the allegation of causing so much harm to his wife that the pregnancy was terminated.

"I deny it," Scott said.

"And do you further deny the allegation alleged as to special circumstances?" she asked, referring to the death penalty part of the charge.

"I also deny it."

The judge and Bazar arranged a bail hearing for May

6—though it would be impossible for him to make bail—and a pre-trial hearing on May 19, a month away. The judge asked Scott if he approved of the dates.

"Yes," he said.

"So we'll set your matter," the judge said repeating the dates for the record, then adding, "And at the present time, Mr. Peterson is being held without bail."

Afterwards, District Attorney James Brazelton told a news conference that no decision had been made yet on the death penalty, but the evidence against Scott was solid. "I wouldn't have issued a complaint if I wasn't confident that we could proceed with the case," he said. He refused to call it a "slam-dunk" as the attorney general had, but said the evidence would be both direct and circumstantial and was "quite voluminous."

Brazelton was keeping it a closely guarded secret what this evidence was, but one new clue came from the criminal complaint and supporting documentation that prosecutors had filed. In a form called a Pre-Booking/Probable Cause Declaration, lead investigator Detective Craig Grogan put in the box marked "Location of offense" this address: 523 Covena Ave., Modesto.

The home of Scott and Laci Peterson.

This strongly suggested that police believed Laci had been killed in her own home.

What's more, in the box for "Date and Time of Offense," Grogan put in two dates: 12/23/02 and 12/24/02, the same notation as on the arrest warrant. Authorities were pursuing the possibility that Laci had been killed as early as the night before she was reported missing—

perhaps shortly after she finished with her phone call to her mother at 8:30 p.m. Her body could have been dumped in the bay any time that night or early in the morning. It raised the question: how many trips did Scott take to the bay?

As Brazelton spoke to reporters, Laci's mother, father and stepfather walked two blocks from the courthouse to an auditorium.

There, they would hold their own press conference, the first since Scott's arrest and the positive identification of Laci's body.

That they felt they needed to say anything at all to the public spoke volumes about the nature of the Laci Peterson case—about the intimate link between private and public. The family had gone to the public in the hopes that getting the word out would help find Laci safe and sound. When the case was changed to a homicide investigation, the aim was to seek the public's help in finding her body.

Now, the public announcement served as a form of therapy—group therapy.

The public had become their family, and they wanted to speak with them directly.

And feel something back.

It would take all the powers of professionalism for the dozens of reporters in attendance to keep their emotions in check.

Before it was over, many of them wept openly.

Laci's father, Dennis Rocha, spoke first—or tried to speak. His words engulfed by tears, he sputtered out thank-yous to the people who supported the family, then said, "Now, justice can be done."

Next to the microphones was Laci's stepfather. "The last four months have been the worst time of our lives," he said. "I've watched our family and friends change both physically and mentally, but one thing that has never changed was that we would do anything within our power to get Laci back. Hundreds of people worked day and night, Christmas, New Year's. Whatever it took, they would do to help find Laci."

He noted the business people who donated materials, the police who "worked day and night," and the media, which "got the word out to the whole nation. He thanked the "people everywhere" for their prayers, cards, e-mails and donations. "We would like to thank all of the people who helped us with our extensive search efforts; those who searched by plane, on horseback, by boat, by car and on foot, as well as divers used in lakes and rivers in several counties surrounding the Modesto area," he said. Calling Kim Petersen and the Sund/Carrington Foundation a "Godsend," he thanked Petersen for her "advice, guidance and support on so many things. She's a part of our lives now."

Then, he moved to the more delicate subject. "I know all of you would like for us to say something about Scott, but we're not going to do that," he said. "We owe it to Laci to let the courts bring the facts out. I'm not going to say anything that could jeopardize the hard work of so many men and women."

There would be no angry denouncements, no comparisons to the Nazis.

Instead, just sadness.

"We started this nightmare with one purpose in mind—to find Laci and bring her home," he said. "While this is not the way we wanted to bring her home, it will help us to begin the long process of healing. While we understand that there are many people who would like to hear from us, in the very near future we have two very tough days to get through." The first was what would have been Laci's 28th birthday, on May 4—thirteen days away. The next was the day of the funeral service for Laci and Conner. The date had not yet been set.

"We realize that we have a very long and difficult road ahead of us and our primary concern is working through this as a family," he said. "All of the cards, flowers, candles, stuffed animals and pictures left at Laci's house mean so much to us. We spend time each day reading the notes and cards left at the house as well as the guestbook entries on the Web site. We have seen video and pictures of many of you stopping by Laci's house to show your support for our family and your love for our Laci and Conner."

He said the stuffed animals would be sent to a center for abused children "in Laci's name."

Finally, with just a hint of defiance, he said, "I feel sorry for Jackie and Lee and their family. They don't deserve this. But Laci and our family don't either."

Laci's longtime friend, Rene Tomlinson, who shared high school years and slumber parties, then dinner parties as they grew older, was the next to speak, and she spoke of Conner. "Now, we will never know his face, never see his smile and never hear his cry," she said in an unsteady voice. "We can only find comfort knowing they will always be together and that Laci is with her son that she loved so much."

Sharon Rocha was next. Laci's mother had spent all night working on what she would say.

"Words alone are not enough to express our sincere gratitude and appreciation to every person and entity that helped in our search for Laci and Conner," she began. "We are very fortunate to live in a community that has come together and supported us from the very beginning of our nightmare and continues to do so. We thank the media for your help and support. Through you, we have been given the opportunity to share our Laci and Conner with people all around the world." She went on to thank the fire departments and the Coast Guard for looking for Laci, Brad Saltzman and the Red Lion Hotel for donating the time and facilities for the search center, the businesses that donated supplies and food, Jonathan Smith for building and maintaining the Laci Peterson Web site, and "to all of those who prayed for us and for the safe return of Laci and Conner."

Then, in stark contrast to the bitter words of Scott's parents, she said, "We especially want to thank the Modesto Police Department, and everyone affiliated with them. We cannot thank you enough for giving up your personal lives, for all the long hours and days and weeks you have spent searching for answers to Laci's disappearance, for your kindness and patience with us, for your understanding of our desperation to find Laci. We also want to thank your spouses, many of whom may have spent the Christmas holidays without your husband or wife, because of their dedication to their department and their tireless efforts to find Laci and Conner. We are grateful to you for sharing your loved ones with us during our time of need."

"We want to thank Kim Petersen, and the entire staff of the Carole Sund/Carrington Foundation," she said. "They have worked diligently to help us inform the public, both locally and nationally, of Laci's disappearance in order to solicit their help in locating her. Due to Kim's experience with situations such as ours, she is familiar with the ups and downs, the highs and lows and the many different emotions we are experiencing. She has made herself available to us and provided guidance and support to help us get through some of our darkest hours. I consider her a very dear friend and offer my sincere gratitude." She continued: "I highly recommend the Carole Sund/Carrington Foundation to anyone seeking help in finding missing loved ones."

She thanked the people who'd helped with the reward fund and then thanked her family and friends. "You have been with us from the beginning of our long walk down this devastating road," she said. "You offered yourselves to us, to lean on and to help carry the weight of our burden. You have been here to support us, give us strength and to help ease our pain. You gave up your own personal lives to be here with us because you know we need you. Without your love and devotion, we would never be able to face what lies ahead. We are eternally grateful to all of you and we thank you."

She said, "If Laci were here now she would be absolutely amazed at the outpouring of love and concern for her and Conner. I know, in my heart, that she is fully aware of the love we have for her."

After the thanks, Sharon recounted the ordeal she'd faced.

"On December 24, 2002, shortly after 5:15 p.m., I received a phone call and heard the devastating words that would forever change my life: 'Laci's missing.' "

This was the call from Scott. "I knew in my heart that something terrible had happened to my daughter and my grandson," she said, leaning up against her husband. "My world collapsed around me. Since receiving that phone call we have been living a terrible nightmare."

The search began that night, she said, and, "the questions were always there: What has happened to Laci? Where is she? Is she safe? Who took her from me? I made a plea to the person or persons who took her to please, please let her go and send her home to us. We heard nothing. As the days passed I made more pleas, to take her to a hospital, or fire or police station, or tell us where she is so that we could come to her and bring her and her baby home safely. Still, we heard nothing. We searched and searched and searched but still no Laci."

She said, "I love my daughter so much. I miss her every minute of every day. My heart aches for her and Conner. Without them there is a huge void in my life. I literally get sick to my stomach when I allow myself to think about what may have happened to them. No parent should ever have to think about the way their child was murdered. In my mind, I keep hearing Laci say to me,

'Mom, please, find me and Conner and bring us home. I'm scared. Please, don't leave us out here all alone. I want to come home. Please don't stop looking for us.' "

By now, emotion engulfed those assembled. Behind her, family members began to cry. Tears streamed down the faces of reporters, many of whom had been covering the case from the day after Laci disappeared.

"I feel that Laci and Conner could no longer wait to be found. So, last week, they came to us. Laci and Conner left us on Christmas Eve. I know that God has been watching over them. He sent them back to us on Good Friday. Now, we can bring them home where they belong," she continued, her voice turning harder. "Laci and her unborn child did not deserve to die. They certainly did not deserve to be dumped in the bay and sent to a watery grave as though their lives were meaningless. Laci meant the world to me. She was my only daughter. She was my best friend. We miss her beautiful smile, her laughter, her love, her kind and loving ways. I miss seeing her, talking to her and hugging her. We have been deprived of meeting and knowing Laci's son, our grandson and nephew. We will miss them and mourn them for the rest of our lives."

Sharon said that after Laci disappeared, she made a promise to her daughter. Her voice gathering strength, she continued, "If she has been harmed, we will seek justice for her and Conner and make sure that the person responsible for their deaths will be punished. I can only hope that the sound of Laci's voice begging for her life, begging for the life of her unborn child, is heard over and over and over again in the mind of that person every day for the rest of his life. The person responsible should be held accountable and punished for the tragedy and devastation forced upon so many."

Not once in the course of this extraordinary statement did Sharon utter the name Scott Peterson.

CHAPTER 19

On April 16, as the state crime lab was extracting DNA from the two bodies found on the shores of San Francisco Bay, the pundit patrol was out in full force. Without positive ID, but with strong suspicions as to whose bodies they were, there was plenty for the talking heads to talk about. Thoughts and feelings, analysis and suspicion, and brazen speculation spilled from Fox News, MSNBC, CNN, as Greta and Dan and Geraldo and Larry presided over the court of cable opinion. What does this mean for Scott? Is an arrest imminent? If he is arrested, will he be charged with one murder or two? Would he face the death penalty? And where *is* Scott?

One of those offering expert observations was a high-profile Los Angeles–based attorney who had made headlines defending a Hollywood actress against shoplifting charges. In an appearance on Fox's *On the Record with Greta Van Susteren*, Mark Geragos, late of the Winona

Ryder trial, had surveyed the information at hand and observed that Scott Peterson was in deep trouble. "They could get an arrest warrant right now. They could indict him right now," he told Greta. "You'd be hard-pressed to find a prosecutor who couldn't put together an indictment, let alone a conviction." On April 18, he said on *Larry King Live*: "The bodies and the remains are found within one mile or two miles of the very location that [Scott] provided to the police as his alibi. That is devastating."

Soon, however, Geragos would be making a statement of a different sort—not on cable television, but before a Stanislaus County Superior Court judge.

"I was retained by Mr. Peterson's family."

Many roads to the Peterson case seemed to run through Condit Country. This was another one. Among Mark Geragos' many high-profile clients—Ryder, Whitewater figure Susan McDougal, President Clinton's brother Roger and actor Robert Downey, Jr.—was Representative Gary Condit, whom Geragos represented during the Chandra Levy investigation. So like the news people camped in front of the courthouse, Geragos was no stranger to Modesto. But as much as this, it was his punditry that garnered the attention of Scott Peterson's parents—not the actual words, since Geragos called them as he saw them, but the passion behind them. Scott was going to need more than just a competent lawyer and vigorous courtroom advocate. He needed a crusader.

On Tuesday, April 29, two weeks after proclaiming Scott fit for imminent indictment, Geragos was at the Stanislaus County Jail for a noon meeting with Scott's attorney of record, Public Defender Tim Bazar, and Scott himself.

The next night, Geragos appeared on CNN's *Larry King Live*.

"I was tremendously impressed by Scott," he said. "I don't think there's any doubt that I believe in him."

The only doubt seemed to center on who would be paying Geragos—and how much. A solid defense in a capital murder case could cost up to $1 million, including not only the fees of Geragos and his co-counsel but costs for private investigators, scientific experts and expert witnesses. Although he represented McDougal for free, the Peterson family, while not rich, clearly had assets, including the San Diego house worth at least a half million dollars, probably more. In the Larry King appearance, Geragos said, "I would definitely say I'm leaning toward helping him." Geragos said he would "sleep on it" and make a decision by week's end.

On Friday, he announced he was taking the case.

"I'm facing a case where I've been advised by everyone not to take it—told it's career suicide, told I'm clinically insane," Geragos told the *Los Angeles Times*. "I do take seriously the idea that you're not supposed to turn down a case just because of its notoriety."

On the contrary. Armed with a beeper that never sleeps, Geragos has been known to call back reporters within seconds, from his car, courthouse halls, restaurants, TV studios, office or tennis court. His juicy sound bites are the stuff that make TV producers weep. And although he has gained a reputation as a slick Hollywood lawyer—his choice of transportation, a black Porsche, and his many appearances on TV certainly contributed to that—Geragos at his core is a committed advocate, who feels that even the scum of the Earth—indeed, especially the scum of the Earth—deserve the best defense possible. "There's no room for innocence before being proven guilty," he would say. "I'm appalled by it."

This was never so evident as in the Winona Ryder case. Although his client was seen on security video hauling so much designer merchandise out of Saks Fifth Avenue that at one point it literally fell out of her hands, Geragos used a blistering defense—including the suggestion that Ryder was framed by zealous and star-struck security guards—to try to convince the jury to believe him rather than their lying eyes. Although Ryder was convicted of felony grand theft and vandalism, she was acquitted of burglary. She ended up spending not a minute in jail, sentenced instead to community service at an AIDS organization and in other groups, and went back to making movies.

The defense was more effective than anyone perhaps thought possible, and yet Geragos brooded over his failure to spare her a conviction on the two felony charges. He believed after summations that he'd get a hung jury on the other two charges as well, setting the stage for what he'd wanted from the very beginning—a plea agreement on misdemeanor counts.

A product of LA's Loyola University Law School, a factory for criminal lawyers, Geragos had wanted to be a lawyer since he was a 5-year-old tagging along with his father to work at the Los Angeles District Attorney's Office, where Paul Geragos was a prosecutor. Although he can appear heartless in court, Geragos comes from a close Armenian family with strong ties to L.A.'s Armenian community and church. He runs the family business—Geragos & Geragos, the second half of the nameplate belonging to his civil lawyer brother, Matthew—out of a Los Angeles high-rise.

He has many friends in high places, among them Attorney General Bill Lockyer. When Geragos was still in pundit mode, he praised the attorney general's office for quickly turning around DNA evidence to help local law enforcement. In an interview with the *San Francisco Chronicle*, he had called the Peterson case "a wonderful showcase for exactly what it is the AG's office does—why it's such an important job."

And while he can be tough on the opposition in court, Geragos has been known to show a softer side on behalf of a client. He protected Ryder like a mother hen when she was engulfed by TV cameras, one of them injuring her arm. For Susan McDougal, he toiled behind the scenes to improve her jail conditions and helped get her a presidential pardon.

The whole package—sweet to the client, tough in court, comfortable with the media and a fierce advocate—all made him the perfect fit for the Peterson case.

And not a minute too soon.

By the time the Peterson family had retained Geragos, Scott Peterson was getting pounded in the press. The coverage was so extensive that one day, a week before Geragos took over as lawyer, the most-watched show on cable was not programming devoted to the war in Iraq, but Fox News' coverage of the Laci Peterson case. The preponderance of publicity against Scott included coverage of the searches of his house, the disastrous revelation of his affair with Amber Frey, his cringe-invoking interview with Diane Sawyer, his selling of Laci's car, the increasingly angry pronouncements against him by Laci's family and the highly suspicious circumstances of his arrest, including his brother's ID, that wad of ten grand and his bad dye job.

Very little was still known about the physical evidence, but what was known looked bad for Scott, beginning with what Geragos himself had pointed out: the fact that the bodies were found on the shores of the bay where Scott himself had said he'd gone fishing the day his pregnant wife disappeared.

Even the fact that Scott sold fertilizer served as a comic metaphor for such late-night hosts as Jay Leno. Scott's now-vacant house had become a flashpoint for people's anger. "Hang his ass!" one man yelled while driving by the house.

His original lawyer Kirk McAllister had tried to beat back some of the publicity, telling the Associated Press after Scott's arrest: "The police had to make an arrest in this case or they would have looked like *Mayberry RFD*." McAllister also said Scott could explain the ten grand and the dye job—just not right now. "The press wants instant truth," McAllister said. "The police want self-serving truth. Hopefully, there will be a process to get to the whole truth about what happened."

With McAllister playing it conservatively, it was left to Scott's family, particularly his devoted mother, increasingly angry father and outspoken sister Susan to defend him against each wave of negative press. As Geragos would say on *Larry King Live* after meeting with

Scott for the first time, "I think he's already universally been convicted in the court of public opinion . . . I don't think that there's anybody that you can talk to that doesn't just assume he's guilty." Guilty in the public's mind could have ramifications in the courtroom when attorneys try to find an impartial jury. With so much animosity in the air, that was going to be a major challenge.

The bad press was one thing. The stakes inside the courtroom were even higher: Scott was facing the very real possibility that prosecutors would seek the death penalty, though it was not a foregone conclusion what the DA would do. Delicate issues came into play, making the decision a difficult one. On Thursday, April 24, two days after Scott pleaded not guilty at his arraignment, District Attorney James Brazelton let slip which direction the office was leaning. During a videotaping of *The John Walsh Show*, the DA said this was the type of case that "cries out" for the death penalty. "If it was just my decision, I would no doubt seek the death penalty," he said. Brazelton wasn't going to make the decision alone, but also consider the recommendation of a committee of trial lawyers in the DA's office. Brazelton said he also wanted to talk to Laci Peterson's family—"I intend to give the family's opinions a lot of weight," he said—as well as Scott's defense lawyer. He made no mention of talking to Scott's family.

The key consideration was whether to seek a second murder charge against Scott for the death of his unborn son. Multiple murder was the "special circumstance" that made Scott eligible for capital punishment. In California, murder charges can be filed in the deaths of fetuses older than seven weeks; with Scott's baby at near term, the statute clearly applied. The statute had resulted from a 1969 beating of an eight-month-pregnant woman by a jealous ex-husband. After being kicked in the stomach and knocked unconscious, the woman was taken to the hospital where doctors delivered a stillborn girl with a cracked skull. In that case, prosecutors charged the man with murder for the baby girl, but the state supreme court threw out the charge on the grounds that only a human "born alive" could be murdered. The legislature passed a new murder law for fetuses, which, with some modifications, passed high-court muster.

On Friday, April 25, Brazelton did in fact meet with Laci's parents. What they said to him wasn't revealed, but they would later make it crystal clear how they felt about the death of baby Conner. In the weeks ahead, they would become strong proponents of legislation to make it a federal crime to kill a fetus, backing a controversial bill called the Unborn Victims of Violence Act. "As the family of Laci Peterson and her unborn son, Conner, this bill is very close to our hearts," the family wrote in a letter to lawmakers. "We have not only lost our future with our daughter and sister, but with our grandson and nephew as well." Such legislation floundered for years in the face of strong opposition from abortion rights groups. Now renamed "Laci and Conner's Law," it had new momentum, much to the chagrin of abortion rights activists. Kate Michelman, president of NARAL Pro-Choice America, told the Associated Press that placing the names of Laci and Conner on the bill was pure exploitation. "It sickens me," she said.

After speaking with Laci's family and considering the

views of the lawyer panel, the Stanislaus County District Attorney's Office announced its decision.

It would seek the death penalty against Scott Peterson in the deaths of both Laci and the baby.

If convicted, Scott could be sentenced to die by lethal injection.

The decision came unusually quickly. Normally, prosecutors wait until after the preliminary hearing, when they must convince a judge they have enough evidence to support a charge. Brazelton would ask for the death penalty.

The reasons why death was opted also weren't entirely known, but Brazelton's statements in the days before, and the position that Laci's family took on the baby's death, certainly provided strong clues. This case was heinous, involving an eight-months-pregnant woman who was also the defendant's wife. The DA's office may also have considered Scott's actions and attitudes after Laci disappeared, including his apparent arrogance and what could be construed as lack of cooperation with police. Working under the assumption that Scott was guilty, prosecutors could believe that Scott, in refusing to divulge the location of Laci's body, prolonged the grief of the family, and the community, and cost law-enforcement agencies large amounts of money.

But there were factors weighing against the death penalty that he had to consider, including the fact that Scott had no criminal history and no reported violence against Laci in the past. There were also factors the public didn't know about that may have been considered, including the manner in which Laci was killed—how violent her death was, how much she may have suffered and how long it may have taken.

In any event, the decision made, Scott's life now hung in the balance.

At the time this was going on, Scott was represented by Ken Faulkner of the public defender's office, working with Bazar. Although Faulkner didn't represent starlets and presidential brothers or appear as Larry King's legal pundit, he was no slouch in court. Faulkner had only been a public defender for two years, having worked the previous twenty years as a defense lawyer in private practice. A graduate of L.A.'s Southwestern University School of Law, another California criminal lawyer factory, Faulkner had gone up against Brazelton in the 1991 Salida Massacre case.

In 1990, members of a bizarre paramilitary cult who called themselves "children of Satan" slaughtered three men and a woman in a Salida, California, duplex with knives and baseball bats. Led by the cruelly charismatic Gerald Cruz, cult members were subjected to torture and rape to stay in line, and wrote in their diaries of desecrating graves, bloodletting and witchcraft. Cruz was given a death sentence, as were David Beck and Ricky Vieria, while Jason LaMarsh and Ronald Willey were given sentences of 64 years to life. All the cases are under appeal.

In that case, Faulkner and the defense team were able to get the trial moved out of Stanislaus County—a tactic almost certainly to be attempted in the Peterson case over prosecution's objections. The jury in the new county, Alameda, was tough. One of those getting death was Faulkner's client. Even in defeat, Faulkner was resolute. When Brazelton boasted in *The Modesto Bee* that, "I've tried death penalty cases with Ken Faulkner" and that "his client is on death row," Faulkner shot back: "We're not talking about a sporting event here; we're talking about someone's life."

It was under these circumstances—publicity against Scott, prosecutor oozing with confidence, death penalty looming—that Geragos, at a hearing on Friday, May 2, officially took over from Faulkner as defense attorney.

Despite Brazelton's bravura, he decided against trying the case himself. As courtroom prosecutors, he chose a pair of bespectacled veterans who were as workmanlike as Geragos was flashy. One was Rick Distaso, who had drafted the wiretap instructions and who'd gotten his law degree from Geragos' alma mater, Loyola. He'd worked three years as a lawyer for the JAG, the Army Judge Advocate General's Corps, and prosecutor for Stanislaus County since 1996. The Peterson case was one of three capital murder cases he was handling. Another, coincidentally, involved a man also facing two murder counts in the death of his pregnant wife. Unlike most prosecutors, Distaso also had experience as a criminal defense lawyer.

The other man at the prosecution table was Senior Deputy District Attorney Dave Harris, a California

Western School of Law graduate who had worked for the Stanislaus County DA's Office since 1991, after stints in San Diego and Kings County. He'd had one prior capital case.

The Department 8 courtroom would be packed with family and media, a sight that would become common for all hearings, big and small, in the coming months. On one side of the courtroom, in the front row, sat Sharon Rocha and Laci's siblings, Brent and Amy. Across the aisle sat Scott's sister, Susan Peterson–Caudillo, just behind the defense table. Security was once again tight, with the two-bailiff security team upgraded to eight deputies. Scott's hands were shackled and he wore the garish red jail jumpsuit.

All this was for a fifteen-minute change-of-attorney hearing. The transfer had already been agreed upon by all parties behind closed doors. Still, at the hearing, Stanislaus County Superior Court Judge Al Girolami did wonder aloud who was paying Geragos, since Scott had said at his arraignment that he needed a public defender and was thus assigned Tim Bazar and later Ken Faulkner.

"I was retained by Mr. Peterson's family," Geragos said.

The judge asked Scott if he agreed to have Geragos as his new lawyer.

"Yes, Your Honor," said Scott, the only time he would speak during the brief hearing.

After the hearing, Geragos wasted no time in practicing his particular brand of advocacy. He faced the TV cameras and said that not only did Scott look forward to "proving his innocence," but he looked forward to "finding out who did this to his wife and to his child, Conner." Explaining his apparent about-face, Geragos said, "I think I succumbed to the media buzz."

Although Geragos' statement had echoes of O. J. Simpson's often-lampooned announcement that he would try to find the real killer or killers of his wife Nicole, it was a turning point in the case: The debate shifted toward Geragos' defense tactics—and away from the question of just how guilty Scott really was. On this first day as Scott's lawyer, Geragos made a more subtle, but equally important, move. He asked the judge for Scott to be allowed to wear civilian clothes rather than the red jail jumpsuit—which screamed "Guilty"—and that he be allowed to walk into court free of the shackles. The judge agreed, saying that even though it was common for defendants to wear the jumpsuits in pre-trial hearings, in this case it may taint potential jurors since they could see still photos and TV images of Scott. From that point on, Scott appeared in suits and ties.

Geragos' hiring meant the end of the involvement by Faulkner and the public defender's office. But Kirk McAllister would be rejoining Scott's defense. Although McAllister had been much less outspoken in the months leading up to Scott's arrest, he now joined Geragos in the strong rhetoric. He would tell NBC's *Dateline* that he had quietly conducted a three-month investigation, building evidence in defense of Scott: "It is hard, it is solid, and it shows Scott didn't do it."

The day after the hearing, Scott's father expanded the defense of his son from the courthouse steps to the cable television audience, calling CNN's *Larry King Live* to take on pundit Nancy Grace, accusing her of having a "personal vendetta" against his son and challenging her about what she knew—or did not know—about the case.

"You are just caught up in this thing and there's no room for, you know, innocence until proven guilty," Lee Peterson said, "and I'm just appalled by that."

Grace, a former Atlanta prosecutor, said: "It's my belief that there's a very strong case against Scott."

Peterson accused Grace of "speculating on these facts."

"And you are believing what your son is telling you," she said.

"Please don't interrupt me," Peterson shot back. "You've had your say here for months, and you've crucified my son on national media. And he's a wonderful man. You have no idea of his background and what a wonderful son and wonderful man he is. And you sit there as a judge and jury, I guess, and you're convicting him on the national media, and you should be absolutely ashamed of yourself."

"Sir," Grace said, "I think he should be ashamed of himself, as whoever is responsible for the death of Laci Peterson. I am simply stating what has been leaked or what has been put in formal documents, and if you find them disturbing, I suggest you ask your son about some of them, sir."

Peterson said Scott has a theory about what happened to his wife. "He believes she was snatched off the street, as we all do. That's why the dog was running around in the neighborhood."

He had a final comment for Grace: "Find a little room in your heart to—for innocence, would you please? Don't, don't convict him over the airwaves. Please. Thank you."

CHAPTER 20

"This is not a rock concert," the man bellowed to the crowd through a bullhorn. "Please enter the building in an orderly fashion."

On a crisp, blustery spring day, about 3,000 people had turned out. They waited outside in two orderly lines, each a block long. At 2:35 p.m., the doors were opened, and the crowd filed into the First Baptist Church of Modesto's cavernous sanctuary. Within minutes the pews were full and 1,000 people couldn't get inside. They were directed to another building to watch on closed-circuit television.

Laci Peterson's family was Catholic, not Baptist, but so many people attended the service on Sunday, May 4—on what would have been Laci's 28th birthday—that denominational lines were erased in the name of crowd control.

And although it wasn't a rock concert, it was on rock concert scale. There was a full orchestra and a choir of

150 singers in white robes, its members drawn from the choirs of both the First Baptist Church and the Big Valley Grace Community Church, standing on a riser in front of white cloth curtains bathed in blue light. The crucifix behind the choir was big. The picture of Laci facing the pews was big. The crowd was big. The audience for this live televised event was big.

So big that it would later be noted that the memorial service beat the previous Modesto record for public grieving for a murdered young woman. Chandra Levy's tribute at Modesto's Centre Plaza almost exactly a year before had drawn 1,200 people.

And like Chandra's memorial, this was one was filled with music and remembrances and the notable—and total—absence of any mention of one particular man.

The program for Laci's memorial set the tone for the service. It read: "Celebrating the life of Laci Rocha Peterson" and it had a picture of a smiling Laci in black with a silver crucifix.

When Laci's mother, Sharon, was pregnant with her, she hoped for a girl. Sharon could already tell Laci was going to be a good baby. Laci was born on May 4, 1975, weighing only six pounds but full of life and happiness. From the time Laci was a baby she woke each morning with a smile on her face, the beautiful smile we have all come to know. Laci grew up to be energetic, imaginative, creative and busy. She always had a project in the works.

As an adult, Laci brought so much to everyone,

her love of good food, fine wine, gardening, entertaining, and to always have a good time in any situation. Laci not only taught her friends proper etiquette but how to laugh; and not just giggle but to laugh loud and often. Laci made sure birthdays were special for her friends and family, whether it was a beautifully baked cake, a few hours of pampering or a special gift waiting on the porch.

For those fortunate enough to have had Laci in their lives, she leaves behind a legacy of wonderful memories for her family and friends to cherish and hold very close to their hearts.

The memorial was held just three weeks after the bodies of Laci and Conner were found, and just two weeks after Scott was arrested for murder. The strain showed on the faces of Laci's family members as they entered the church. They took off their sunglasses to reveal red watery eyes.

Sharon Rocha, Dennis Rocha, Ron Grantski, Amy Rocha and Brent Rocha took their seats in the front row. Before them stood the choir and the blown up picture of Laci with her famously broad smile. The portrait of the woman who'd once studied ornamental horticulture was surrounded by flowers in red, pink and white. There was a white bouquet shaped like a heart with a line of red petals down the middle: a broken heart. For Conner, there was a white column holding the figurine of a child next to white roses.

Behind Laci's family was a sanctuary filled with thousands, each mourner wearing ribbons of blue and yellow, just like those worn at the candlelight vigil in the soggy park a week after Laci had disappeared, when everybody still held hope that she would be found alive.

Laci's image flashed on huge video screens while a recording of Sarah McLachlan's "I Will Remember You" filled the church. The photos were heartbreaking: Laci as a little girl, Laci with her Christmas bike, Laci laughing at a Halloween party, Laci standing next to Brent in his soccer uniform, Laci as a cheerleader, Laci dressed up for a formal dance in a white party dress and big hair, Laci goofing with her girlfriends.

Then there were the pictures from her adult years: Laci on her wedding day, Laci dancing in her white wedding gown, Laci pregnant with Conner.

Those who had followed the news carefully knew that something was missing. The tall, handsome husband who'd shared these moments with her had been carefully and deliberately cropped from the pictures, from her life.

Nobody uttered Scott's name, but one woman shouted from the balcony, "God will judge whoever took Laci!"

Only one person from Laci's family spoke to the crowd, brother Brent. Laci's mother stayed with the other family members, dabbing tears.

"Today is a good day," said Brent, dressed in a dark suit, clutching the program with Laci's smiling face. "Today is Laci's birthday. All of us are given an opportunity to remember Laci and Conner. Laci would be very grateful and just astounded that she would get this kind of attention. I think with all of us here, we're sending a very powerful message."

Fighting tears, Brent told a story about the day his family had a funeral for his grandmother, and how Laci said that at her funeral: "I don't want people to be sad.

I don't want them to be missing me. I want them to be happy."

Brent looked at the thousands and said, "I'm here today to convey that message for her.

"She would be grateful and astounded," he said. "She would not believe all of this would happen for her. . . . Laci would say, 'Nah-uh—all of this isn't happening for me.' She's going to be dearly missed."

Four friends were listed on the program to speak; eight did. They spoke of the time a little girl had jumped in the pool naked at her brother's dare, of karaoke and slumber parties, of making commercial re-enactments, of dinner parties that required the best clothes, and of Laci's glorious pregnancy—how she wore maternity clothes at three months and barely showing. One friend said she pictured Laci and Conner in heaven, holding hands, wearing wings of gold.

"We are all better people for having known Laci," said friend Kim McNeely. "I take comfort in knowing that Laci and Conner are together, and the same smile that I will miss every day is now shining down on us through heaven."

Another friend noted that Laci was the consummate party planner, whose dinners were admired by her friends. Her disappearance drew the community closer. "What an incredible hostess she turned out to be," said Heather Sutton.

The service, which had been filled with Christian hymns sung by the orchestra-backed choir, ended with a pop song. Van Morrison's "Brown Eyed Girl" had been Laci's favorite song, and as it played in the First Baptist Church of Modesto, five months of worry, anticipation, frustration, anger, bitterness and betrayal erupted into a single tearful outpouring of emotion.

The choir began singing the song.

Then the thousands in the sanctuary sang and clapped and cried.

When it was over, the mourners filed out past Laci's portrait to pay their respects. Some said a prayer. Others left a flower. Some stroked their hands across the photo.

A few blocks away, the man who had been edited out of Laci's photographic history huddled with his new attorney, Mark Geragos, at the jail for more than five hours. Although the service was televised live, Scott and the lawyer were in a TV-less room. By now, Scott's fate was completely at the mercy of the justice system, his day-to-day affairs no longer his concern. He had transferred power of attorney to his parents. His pets were in the care of others. McKenzie, the golden retriever Laci was to walk the morning she disappeared, was with Scott's family in San Diego. The cats, Siam and Gracie, were going to be cared for by a friend of Laci's.

As remarkable as it seems, Scott had actually shown some interest in attending the service. He asked his sheriff's department jailers how he could get a pass. The department had been known to let inmates attend funerals, as long as they pay for the extra security costs for guards. In the end, Scott never actually applied for the pass. It would have done no good. The sheriff said that Scott was an inmate under the control of Stanislaus County and he wasn't going anywhere outside the jail walls except for court.

Scott wasn't the only person absent. Amber Frey said through her father that she had been invited, but declined to go, citing what would almost certainly be a media circus that would strip the event of its dignity. Scott's parents also didn't go to the service. Jackie had called Laci's mother to tell her that she, too, wanted to see the kind of peaceful, proper service that might not be possible if they or any members of the Peterson family attended. So they all stayed home. "We will grieve in our own private way with Scott," Lee told *The Modesto Bee*, "because we all loved Laci."

But over the next four months, as the crisp spring in the Central Valley turned to a scorching hot summer, the celebration of Laci Peterson on display at the First Baptist Church would be eclipsed by bitter fighting.

The world had seen Modesto at its finest. Now, another side would be exposed.

CHAPTER 21

If nothing else, Scott didn't look as guilty as he had before. Gone were the red jumpsuit and shackles, replaced by a nicely tailored blue suit, white shirt and tie. His blond-dyed hair was starting to turn back to its normal brown.

The day after the memorial service, on Monday, May 5, Scott Peterson made his first court appearance since Mark Geragos had taken over as defense lawyer, one of what would be many sessions dealing with procedural issues and legal wrangling, but not the evidence.

That would have to wait until the preliminary hearing.

The issue at hand was who was going to preside over matters relating to the Peterson case. Already, there were two judges. Superior Court Judge Al Girolami was handling the criminal case against Scott. Judge Roger M. Beauchesne was presiding over a debate on whether to unseal the search warrant affidavits and other documents containing juicy information about why authorities thought Scott Peterson had murdered his wife.

Until now, despite massive media attention, precious little was known about the evidence the prosecution had against Scott. In one of the few areas where they would agree, both the defense and the prosecution wanted these documents kept from the prying eyes of reporters, whose organizations would repeatedly push for access to the autopsy reports and search warrant affidavits, and be repeatedly rebuffed.

Scott's lawyers went one step further, and wanted one judge, not two, to be handling both Scott's criminal case and the civil court dispute over the documents, calling the two cases intertwined and in need of a single arbiter of justice. But Judge Girolami said that since the cases involved separate issues and separate parities they would remain separate, and Girolami would continue to be the judge in the criminal side of the case.

A former Stanislaus County prosecutor, insurance claims adjuster and Army lieutenant, Girolami had been a judge for nineteen years and presided over trials involving the usual criminal mayhem of modern society, from murderers to a grandmother accused of stealing a library's stash of late-fines money—$80,000 worth. Girolami was the prototypical no-nonsense judge—patient even in the face of Geragos' most outlandish outbursts, impatient with lawyers who dared to speak longer than allowed. He ran his courtroom quietly but firmly.

In addition to keeping himself on the case, Girolami ordered that the Contra Costa County coroner would keep custody of the bodies of Laci and the baby even though the autopsies were complete. Judges typically do this to give the defense team time to examine the bodies, though Laci's family would come to be shocked at just how long the bodies would be stashed away at the coroner's office in Martinez.

A proper Christian burial would have to wait so Scott could get justice.

These two early hearings were marked as much by the sideshow theatrics of the defense as the substantive issues being litigated. During one hearing, Geragos said he had received 6,000 pages of documents from the prosecution and found them "rife with inadmissible evidence, with voodoo-type of investigation, with psychics, voice-stress analyzers, people who study facial expressions—all of which is inadmissible in court." Then, outside of court, Geragos would continue to pound on what would become the defense theme. He vowed to "find out who did this to Scott's wife and Scott's son."

No matter that Geragos failed to elaborate on how he knew there was another killer or killers out there, and if so, why his client was still incarcerated? The media was gobbling it up.

This suburban true-crime drama unfolding in Modesto continued to draw huge ratings on cable television and generated articles in national publications, including *Time, Newsweek, People* and the supermarket tabloids. The media was now a permanent fixture in Modesto. The bars and restaurants and hotels reaped the benefits of the expense-account-covered activities of the visiting press, even as Scott's old neighbors on Covena Avenue grew disgusted with the constant door-knocking by reporters asking them the same questions they'd answered dozens of times going on five months now. Residents of the La Loma neighborhood complained that the noisy satellite trucks rumbled in at all hours and stayed late at night. Some neighbors started posting "No reporters" signs on their doors and stopped answering their phones.

But each day brought even more signs that the reporters weren't going away any time soon. In addition to the unfolding courtroom melodrama, there were developments to the west in the month of May, as the search boats and divers returned to the San Francisco Bay. Police wouldn't say what they were looking for. One diver was seen photographing a chunk of concrete and a length of rope on the shoreline. The flotilla of search boats, including a Coast Guard boat for security, did stick to the same area off Richmond where the bodies were found.

On the legal front, mid-May brought word that another legal celebrity was joining the fray. Amber Frey hired Los Angeles attorney and cable news pundit Gloria Allred. Allred swiftly called a news conference in LA to announce her own hiring and to trot out a newly made-over Amber, sporting feathered hair and a conservative turtleneck with jacket. Since her last news conference had rocked the case, anticipation was high that Amber would give the reporters something new. They would be disappointed.

"I want to express my sympathy to Laci's family," Amber told reporters on May 19, reading from a statement. "My heart goes out to them for the terrible loss of their daughter and grandson. I am grateful that Gloria Allred has agreed to represent me as my attorney. This has been a painful and stressful time for me and I really appreciate her support."

Then, after the plug, she said, "I expect that I will be

asked to testify in this case, and I am prepared to do so. I don't think it's appropriate to talk about what might be contained in my testimony prior to my being called to the witness stand. Until that time, I just want to lead a normal life and regain my privacy. I hope that everyone will understand and respect my wishes."

And that was it. No word on what that testimony would be about. Nothing about Scott or the affair.

Allred then spoke. She said that Amber was not only a witness in the case, but "is also a victim of Scott's deception" and that "we are committed to protecting the integrity of the prosecution, and we will not allow her testimony to be contaminated by offers of money for her story."

While the second Amber press conference produced more flash than substance, there was no shortage of scoops to be found. NBC got a good one when it reported on May 13 that police had found pliers with strands of hair stashed under a seat in Scott's boat. Sources would later say that examiners couldn't rule out whether this was Laci's hair, though it wasn't a match to Scott's.

TV station KTVU reported the same day that the burglary across the street from the Peterson house may have been more relevant to Laci's disappearance than previously suggested—though not in the way that Scott's family had hoped. The station said that the prosecution may call as a witness one of the burglary suspects who had been casing the Petersons' street on Christmas Eve and who saw Scott acting suspiciously. The station also reported that police believed Scott had actually made two trips to Berkeley Marina on December 24, once before dawn, then another time later in the morning when he said he had gone.

The month of May ended with the biggest media "get" of all, when Dan Abrams of MSNBC reported portions of the autopsy report, including the provocative detail about 1½ loops of tape found wrapped around the fetus' neck, and the gash to the baby's torso. ABC and the Associated Press would also reveal sketchy details from the reports. Although a journalistic coup, the information shocked Laci's family. "No family should ever have to learn the autopsy results of somebody they love on national TV," said spokeswoman Kim Petersen.

With fresh details emerging from the autopsy reports, the cable punditry corps went into spasms of speculation, wondering who had leaked them—and who would benefit by it.

In Modesto, prosecutors thought they knew. "The information being leaked has clearly been skewed in favor of the defense," they said in court papers. And for this reason, the prosecution made a bold recommendation: release the entire autopsy report.

This position ran contrary to the say-nothing stance of both police and the district attorney's office on matters relating to the evidence. While neither confirming nor denying the information that had been leaked, in the papers filed by Senior Deputy District Attorney Davis Harris, prosecutors said, "The People believe that releasing the autopsy reports will protect its client, namely the people of the state of California."

An indignant Geragos responded, "I don't know who they got the document from and I certainly didn't want the document public." He said he would be "very happy" to put Abrams on the witness stand, waive any attorney–client privilege between Geragos and Scott and "ask him if he got this information from me." To the prosecution, Geragos said, "I challenge them to do same."

This sort of bickering is to be expected by professional litigators. But by the end of May, the squabbling spilled outside the courtroom.

It would become one of the sadder spectacles of the case, one that all sides would hope would not be repeated. For some time, a dispute had been brewing over what to do with the Covena Avenue home and all the stuff inside. The house was something of a time capsule, frozen the morning that Laci disappeared. Whatever had left the house was taken by search warrant by police. The rest stayed in place, at the request of lawyers and authorities, in case additional searches were needed. Meanwhile, with Laci dead and Scott in jail, the house was going to pot. Plants were dying. Vandals were taking things. Laci's dream house was getting to be an eyesore.

On Wednesday, May 28, Laci's family announced that all this would change. They had hired an attorney to arrange for the family to get inside the house and retrieve belongings with sentimental value. The statement included a twenty-two-point list of Rocha family demands. They wanted such items as Laci's diplomas and journals, two Tiffany lamps and a watering can that read "Laci's Garden." They wanted the right to go into the never-used nursery with the nautical theme and "sit in Conner's room in the rocking chair Laci had purchased to rock him in, and just to have the opportunity to feel her presence," the family statement said. Then, the Rochas wanted to take away the rocking chair, and the crib, among other baby items.

The lawyer had been called in because the Rochas had no access to the house. Scott's mother had changed the locks and alarm code. When the Rocha family asked Jackie for the new code and key, they never got a reply, they claimed. According to the Rochas, they tried to work with Mark Geragos to get some of the belongings, but that he only wrote back to snippily say it would be "unthinkable to allow anything to be moved or disposed of" until the defense team finished its own investigation, including going through the house.

The situation deteriorated into a petty he-said, she-said squabble, with Jackie Peterson contending it was Scott's family, not Laci's, that was working to keep the house clean and the yard tidy, even though they live in San Diego, and that it was being so neglected that items were disappearing, including loose bricks from the patio project, a pair of glass hurricane lanterns and a patio chess set with marble playing pieces shaped like frogs. Geragos told *The Modesto Bee* he was trying to wrap up the defense inventory of the house within ten days. "It's an awful situation," he said, "and we're going to work our way through it with as much dignity as we can. There are two families here who have lost a grandson."

But two days after the Rocha family released its statement, all dignity went out the window. On the morning of Friday, May 30, Laci's family and friends arrived at the house in a caravan of cars and pickups. They went inside, triggering the alarm. Then, as television cameras broadcast live, they proceeded to remove from the house furniture and personal items, including the baby crib. Laci's brother was seen loading the rocking chair into the back of a pickup.

The alarm brought to the scene police officers and a defense attorney, Matthew Dalton, who had to ask reporters what was going on. Police responded to the security company's call at about 10 a.m., hung around for a while, then left without arresting anybody, considering the situation a civil, not criminal, matter.

It was left to a Rocha family attorney, now also on the scene, to try to explain the situation as best he could, saying the Rochas had been in contact with Scott's lawyers and that everything that was being hauled off was being videotaped. "I apologize for it coming down to this," said lawyer Adam Stewart. "This is not the way we operate. It's depressing that it's come down to this." But it was necessary, he said. "We weren't getting anything done," he said.

An angry Jackie Peterson later told reporters that the Rochas had "absolutely no permission" to go into the house. Although the Rochas had now reduced their twenty-two-point list to sixteen items, there were things she just wasn't going to give them, including Laci's wedding ring, another diamond ring and some loose gems that Laci and Scott were going to mount in a new ring, *The Modesto Bee* reported. She also didn't want the Rochas to have the glass memento box she had given Scott and Laci—the one they'd put the shells in from their honeymoon in Tahiti. Jackie complained that Laci's family was taking baby stuff—clothes, toys, the rocking chair, the crib—even though Scott's family had bought nearly all of it as shower gifts. She had already conceded to Brent Rocha the flower vase wall sconces that he had given to Laci, and to Amy Rocha the wicker furniture from Laci's grandmother. But Jackie said her son didn't want to part with the cookbooks, food processor and blender because he needed those to "keep house." He did agree the kitchen could do without the snail-motif salt and pepper shakers.

And so it went, until finally the families resolved the property dispute behind closed doors, who getting what being left mercifully private, the issue never to surface again—which was all very well, because Scott's defense attorneys had more important things to worry about than who got the snail salt-and-pepper shakers.

They had just found out that Scott's phones had been tapped.

CHAPTER 22

Sometimes a criminal defense lawyer's anger and indignation seem contrived for the benefit of the client.

And sometimes they can seem genuine.

Such was the case when Kirk McAllister reacted to the revelation that conversations he'd thought he was having in total confidence with his client, Scott Peterson, were being monitored by agents from the California Department of Justice. One of those agents, he said incredulously, he had known for twenty years and "he didn't recognize my voice?"

Overall, the defense learned, agents "intercepted" 3,858 phone calls—sixty-nine of them between Scott and McAllister and another two between Scott and a private investigator. Although prosecutors would claim that intercepting a call is not the same as listening to a call—and that only a couple of these calls were actually listened to or recorded, and then only for seconds—McAllister was beside himself. He simply couldn't believe it when he heard that part of one of his conversations was overheard by this agent because the agent didn't realize that Scott was talking to a lawyer.

It wasn't just Scott's conversations with his attorneys and investigator that authorities heard. Scott's conversations with Amber were also monitored, and the defense was suddenly faced with the realization that Scott had continued to talk to Amber not only after Laci disappeared, but after Amber went public.

Also monitored were Scott's conversations with the news media. Reporters were heard working one source—Scott Peterson—while another source, the DA's office, was listening. When the tapes went to the defense team, then they too would hear the reporters in action.

As unsettling as the wiretapping was, the situation did present a golden opportunity for Scott. This was the first occasion that the defense could challenge evidence against him, as well as shift the public debate further away from Scott's character and possible guilt to the police tactics.

On Tuesday, May 27, Judge Al Girolami held a hearing on whether to give Scott's attorneys the tapes of seventy-one monitored conversations between Scott and his defense team. Appearing in court, Scott sported yet another look: he had a buzz cut, leaving bristles of brown hair and none of the blond from the dye. He had on another suit, this one light gray. Behind him sat his parents Lee and Jackie, and at one point he turned and nodded toward them. He didn't acknowledge Laci's family, who were also in the courtroom.

In the long, dry, two-hour hearing, during which Scott showed no emotion, the defense told the judge it needed the tapes to see if authorities had overstepped their legal bounds by improperly monitoring privileged communication between client and counsel, and, if so, whether some sort of action should be taken, from sanctions to exclusion of evidence. Prosecutors had acknowledged that a couple of calls between Scott and McAllister were recorded by accident, but in court, prosecutor Rick Distaso, who had written the wiretap instructions, insisted "we're probably talking about two minutes or less" of conversation. And, he claimed, nobody from the DA's office had listened to the tapes anyway.

Judge Girolami agreed to give the defense lawyers the tapes, which they listened to and—to nobody's surprise—were left with outrage. On Monday, June 2, as tensions were smoldering—this was three days after Laci's family and friends had picked up the effects from Scott and Laci's house—Scott's lawyers accused authorities of "grave prosecutorial misconduct" because of "illegal eavesdropping" of "totally privileged" attorney–client communications. The defense contended that prosecutors improperly instructed the wiretap monitors to "intermittently listen in" on calls between Scott and his attorney, "purportedly in reliance" on the Penal Code section that outlines the rules for wiretapping. The defense said this was bad enough, but the wrongdoing was "further compounded" by the monitors' failure to follow the rules and instead spot-check attorney–client conversations up to four times as frequently as the state law allowed.

Scott's lawyers called for a closed-door hearing to address the allegations and possibly question, under oath, prosecutor Distaso and the investigators who'd listened to the conversations. If, as the defense believed, it turned out that prosecutors did improperly handle the wiretaps, the defense suggested a number of sanctions, from throwing the DA's office off the case to excluding not only the testimony of those involved in the wiretapping, but any evidence that might have been collected as a result of the eavesdropping. In the case of Amber Frey, this evidence could be substantial.

Prosecutors responded with a meaty 36-page brief defending its wiretapping activities, asserting that only three of the seventy-one calls between Scott and McAllister or the defense investigator were either listened to or recorded. Prosecutors insisted that while the wire monitors may have picked up scraps of details from these calls of only a few seconds concerning innocuous subjects, none of the prosecutors themselves had listened to these conversations and didn't intend to.

"Over the course of approximately 30 days, through the conduct of two wiretaps and 3,858 intercepted phone calls, the defense can only argue over three," prosecutor Rick Distaso wrote in the papers. "That fact alone should tell the court that the agents acted completely properly through the course of both wiretaps."

Prosecutors disputed the defense claim that monitors listened to more than fifty privileged calls, saying the prosecution "can only surmise that the defendant's complaint involves the initial monitoring of any calls to determine the identity of the parties involved. Such conduct is clearly permitted."

The moment the monitors recognized an attorney's voice, they stopped monitoring, the prosecution said.

Distaso bristled at the notion that any sanctions should be imposed. "While the defense apparently desires to influence the court with inflammatory language, noticeably lacking from their submission is any [legal] case relating to the conduct of wiretaps," the prosecutor wrote. In short, Geragos was offering hot air, but no legal reason to punish the prosecution. "The defense has not been able to make any showing of prejudice in this case," he wrote. "The court can review exactly what happened for all attorney calls. . . . Upon such a review the court will find that no misconduct occurred, and no prejudice resulted to the defendant."

The prosecution would lose some of its moral high ground days later when they revealed that investigators had stumbled onto recordings of portions of *another* 176 tapped calls. Having already acknowledged overhearing some attorney–client chitchat because the wiretap monitor didn't recognize the attorney's voice, authorities this time blamed what in court papers they called a "peculiarity" in AT&T's cell phone technology. This anomaly, they said, allows calls to be recorded without telling the wiretap monitors of this recording. Authorities insisted, again, that nothing of any importance was picked up— mainly dial tones and dead air—though monitors did catch about 10 seconds of one conversation, apparently a business call between Scott and a man with a Southern drawl.

Still, it was nothing if not an embarrassment for the district attorney's office. How many more "peculiarities" would it take before the judge would wonder just how completely proper the wiretap operation really was?

While the defense and prosecution butted heads over the wiretaps, another problem arose for Scott's camp, one that cut to the very heart of Mark Geragos' defense strategy.

Judge Girolami was getting impatient: the autopsy leaks, the press conferences on the courthouse steps, all that incessant chatter about all things Peterson seemed to rankle the mild-mannered former insurance claims adjuster. And he was no foe of the media. He had allowed cameras in his courtroom, which many judges in the post-O. J. environment won't do.

The judge was considering a gag order.

As soon as the judge floated the idea of some sort of protective order, the defense reeled. Scott's lawyers already were working under a strict sealing order—the autopsy reports, police documents, search warrants and other documents were all being kept away from public view, despite numerous challenges by lawyers for the news media. Lawyers were still allowed to talk about other issues, but even with Geragos' best spin doctoring, a survey taken a month after he was hired found that nearly 60 percent of the Stanislaus County residents polled believed that Scott was "probably guilty" or "guilty beyond a reasonable doubt." This may well have been an improvement over people thinking he was guilty as sin just a few weeks earlier. Still, only 3 percent thought he was innocent and more than half the people thought he should get the death penalty if found guilty, according to the survey of 150 people by criminal justice professor Stephen Schoenthaler of California State University, Stanislaus. That sliver of people thinking he was innocent was particularly disturbing since, in the eyes of the law, Scott technically was innocent, as all defendants are, until proven guilty beyond a reasonable doubt.

It was only going to get worse, with more damaging information to come when the prosecution laid out its case in a preliminary hearing.

Geragos strongly opposed a gag order.

"Even if the participants are gagged it will do little to stop the tsunami of coverage of this matter," Geragos wrote in court papers. "In fact, it is the position of the defense that a so-called 'gag' order would result in the law of unintended consequences. Namely, all that a 'gag' order would do is increase the breath and depth of misinformation and scurrilous accusations that swirl around this case, with no ability to mitigate the damage."

Amber Frey's attorney, Gloria Allred, also objected to the gag order, saying she needed to be able to speak to protect Amber. "Since this case is the subject of such intense media focus, Ms. Frey has herself become the subject of intense media focus," wrote Allred in court papers. "In particular, real and imagined aspects of her personal life have been, and remain, media fodder." Allred said that "in contrast to the other concerned parties," Amber had only gone to the media twice and "has not accused the defendant of any crime, commented on the merits of the case or disclosed what her potential testimony might be."

Rather, said Allred, Frey went before the cameras the first time, in the memorable January 24 news conference, only because the press had reported "from leaks by others" that Amber was involved in a romantic relationship with Scott. "These reports placed Ms. Frey in a false light, and were damaging to her reputation. The press then sought Ms. Frey out and hounded her relentlessly," said Allred. "To put an end to the media harassment and assaults on her reputation, Ms. Frey decided to make a statement of her own . . . Ms. Frey hoped that after that press conference the press would stop following her and trying to contact her. She also hoped that the press would stop discussing her personal life."

She thought wrong. "The press continued to discuss her personal life and to contact her even though she asserted that she did not wish to make any further comments." The "press intrusion" grew "so intense" that Amber hired Allred as her "attorney and spokesperson," Allred wrote. What's more, "Ms. Frey also retained counsel to respond as necessary to unfair attacks on her reputation and to false statements about her private life." Her only other media appearance, Allred noted, was the news conference to announce Allred's hiring. "Since then," Allred said, "Ms. Frey has not given interviews to the press. Unfortunately, however, the media continue to report rumors about Ms. Frey. Those rumors amount to an assault on her character and reputation." Allred noted that one news source outside reported that Amber was thinking of posing for *Playboy*. A reporter had also asked Allred about rumors that Amber had been convicted of a crime. "Her counsel told the reporter that such rumors were false," said Allred.

"Ms. Frey is not an eyewitness to the murders in question, and is not a witness 'for' any side despite what either side may argue," Allred wrote. "In this regard, it is crucial to note that she does not accuse the defendant of murdering anyone." Allred doesn't say what Scott may or may not have said to Amber about Laci's disappearance, only that Amber felt she possessed "relevant information" in the investigation. "She is, in the final analysis, a private citizen who by cruel circumstances has been dragged into this highly public matter."

Therefore, said Allred, "The imposition of a gag order would render Ms. Frey unable to respond to unfair attacks on her reputation and would do irreparable damage to her. In short, a gag order against Ms. Frey would render her helpless in the face of a continued onslaught of rumor and innuendo. If the price a person may have to pay for providing police with evidence that may be relevant to a criminal investigation in a high-profile case is that the person will be gagged and unable to respond to unjustified attacks on their reputation, then witnesses may be reluctant to step forward and provide law information with relevant information."

The prosecution staked a middle ground in the debate. "In spite of the court's sealing order, information has repeatedly been leaked to the media," prosecutors wrote. "Media reports have occasionally identified which 'side' was the source of their information, but have refused to disclose the source of leaks. Almost all leaks to the media have been false, misleading or biased in some way."

The prosecution then called for an order locking the lips of only the lawyers in the case, investigators and assorted helpers. Noticeably absent was a call for a gag order on the boss or bosses or the lawyers and investigators, allowing people like the chief of police, his spokesman, the District Attorney and his spokespeople, to continue to talk.

"This court has 'sealed' information to prevent release to the public," the prosecution said. "Some of that information has been leaked to the media which has forced the People to respond. The People's response was necessary to mitigate the recent adverse publicity; a broader order would deprive the People of the right to protect its case."

The papers concluded by saying this limited gag order was really in the media's best interest, whether it knew it or not. "It is the People's belief that once an order is put in place, responsible journalists will understand that leaked information violates the court's order and is being spewed forth with an intent to circumvent justice. And if justice cannot protect the defendant, then who will protect the media in the future?"

Both of these issues—the wiretap sanctions and the gag order—along with a host of other matters, including the prosecution request to unseal the autopsy report, all went before Judge Girolami in a hearing on Friday, June 6. His rulings hardly rocked the case. He said the autopsy report would remain sealed, which was not unexpected. He put off deciding on the wiretap sanctions and the gag order.

These legal issues were overshadowed by the emotion on display. As lawyers and the judge discussed the unsealing of the autopsy report, Scott wept at the counsel table. Laci's mother also burst into tears and had to leave the courtroom on the arm of her husband, Ron Grantski. The hearing ended with the judge ordering the Contra Costa County coroner to issue death certificates for Laci and the baby. As he said this, Scott wiped his teary eyes with a handkerchief.

A week later, Judge Girolami delivered his decision on the gag order. For a judge considering the silencing of all involved, he had a lot to say.

Girolami began his June 12 decision by stating the obvious: the Peterson case had attracted a huge amount of national media attention. Everybody from Geraldo Rivera to Katie Couric had gone on the air with tales from the Laci saga, including many interviews from those involved. Police, family members, expert commentators—everyone had weighed in, the judge noted. A Web site set up to distribute court documents and other information to the media received 12,000 hits in the previous four weeks alone. The judge, himself, had allowed cameras into the courtroom, furthering the publicity.

"The nature of the publicity is especially troubling as it often involves leaks of information that could be considered favorable for one side or the other," he wrote, citing the leaked portions of the autopsy report, even though that document was already ordered sealed. He also noted that defense theories had drifted into the media. On the prosecution side, he noted Attorney General Lockyer's "comments" on the "weight of the evidence"—a reference to the "slam-dunk" remark after Scott's arrest.

In deciding whether all this was so bad it warranted a gag order, Judge Girolami looked to the Fugitive—not the Tommy Lee Jones movie, but the real fugitive case:

the 1950s trial of Dr. Sam Sheppard, a trial in which the pre-trial publicity was so out-of-hand that the Supreme Court overturned his conviction in his wife's murder. Sheppard died in 1970. His son mounted a crusade to clear his name, and would later claim that modern science exonerated his father when DNA tests on blood found on Sheppard's pants didn't belong to him.

Proving he was no fan of sequels, Girolami wrote, "If this case were to proceed to trial without a protective order in place until shortly before jury selection, all the statements by the witnesses, all the rumors and gossip would be rehashed shortly before trial, thereby making it extremely difficult to select a fair and impartial jury."

Finding a "clear and present danger" to Scott's fair-trial rights—so clear and so present that not even moving the trial to another county or extensive questioning of potential jurors would help—Girolami issued a sweeping gag order. Attorneys, their staffs, cops, court officials, potential witnesses—all would be barred from commenting on anything more than the weather to reporters. There would be no more talk of evidence, of theories, of witness statements, of Scott's demeanor. Nothing.

Violators will be held in contempt of court.

Lips didn't stay sealed for long.

Within hours, Gloria Allred was on the Fox News show "On the Record" with Greta Van Susteren, talking about a private session that defense had with the judge to go over what the defense found to be evidence of "other suspects" in the case. Allred said the only reason the defense claimed to have this evidence—and wanted the evidence presented in private so as not to alert these suspects—was that it wanted the search warrants to remain sealed.

It wouldn't be Allred's last post–gag order TV appearance. As she told Van Susteren of the order, "I am not covered by it."

Then, a week after the judge's order, an interview with District Attorney Jim Brazelton, whose office had sought a limited gag order, appeared on the front page of *The Modesto Bee* saying the preliminary hearing would feature prosecution evidence "that might open some eyes." He said one of the reasons his office wanted a public preliminary hearing, rather than a closed-door grand jury proceeding to seek an indictment against Scott, was to counter inaccurate reports about the case. "We spend all our time running down this phony-baloney stuff they throw up," he said.

In the post–gag order world, the only one not talking was the guy everybody thought had the biggest mouth of all—Geragos.

Through clenched teeth, he was incensed.

In separate briefs, Geragos said Allred was "mocking the authority of this court," that Brazelton made remarks that were "nothing less than outrageous" and that the gag order should be rescinded.

Judge Girolami ultimately sided with Allred; his sweeping order wasn't so sweeping that it included the lawyers of witnesses. She was allowed to continue talking, and did so, enthusiastically, appearing on TV shows and holding press conferences on the street outside the courthouse. He delayed making a ruling on Brazelton, but that was the last of the DA's comments. In the future, he would send a spokesman to the microphones to utter only gag order–allowed banalities, mostly about courtroom procedure.

As for Geragos, he didn't talk publicly at all.

But details of Scott Peterson's defense would still manage to get out.

CHAPTER 23

Locals call it the Bulb. It's a point of land that sticks into the San Francisco Bay, shaped like a hatchet, with the blade end pointing south and the handle going toward land past the Albany Mud Flats just north of the Golden Gate Fields racetrack, not far from Berkeley. The landscape on the Bulb is wild and weedy, with trails winding through waist-high expanses of licorice-smelling anise and berries. At the northern end of the point, a trail goes down to the shoreline, where the bay waters lap against the rocks and the wind blows hard from the Golden Gate Bridge to the west.

It is there that nature gives way to art.

Strange and disturbing art.

All along the water's edge are paintings on sheets of wood, clumps of concrete and rocks. The pigments are faded by the elements, but the images are unmistakable: tortured souls rising from the flames of hell, a cowering man about to be beheaded, faces frozen in deathly agony. The dominant color is red. In one area, a concrete structure reminiscent of a crypt is lined with paintings on the inner walls above a puddle of rank water.

One picture shows a Satan-like figure with a pitchfork, standing up in a boat in a sea of red stabbing toward ghostly shapes in the waters below. Not far away is a sculpture made out of the severed feet of mannequin.

And in the distance, across a mile of water, lies the Point Isabel Regional Shoreline, where the bodies of Laci and Conner were found.

Laci, whose remains washed ashore with severed feet.

Scott Peterson's defense team would place floats in the water off the Bulb. The floats would bob across the bay on the currents and winds to Richmond Inner Harbor, just north of where the bodies were discovered.

The defense would theorize that the bodies could have been dumped at this scene of horror and depravity.

The nation would come to know about this theory because it was on the front page of *The Modesto Bee* on August 13, accompanied by a photo of a defense attorney briefing two defense-hired forensic experts, Drs. Henry Lee and Cyril Wecht, at the state forensics lab in Ripon. The gag order was in full force, and defense lawyer Mark Geragos would contend that the reporter and photographer from the *Bee* eavesdropped on a private conversation conducted while the defense team members were cooling their heels and talking about the devil. The *Bee* countered that not only were the men fully aware they were being watched and listened to, the reporter even walked up and introduced himself.

Whether it was press spying or a clever defense move to circumvent the gag order, the story got out there, highlighting a key part of Scott Peterson's game plan to defend himself against murder charges: the Satanic cult theory.

No matter that some of the artists responsible for the works quickly denied being part of any Satanic organization, or even being influenced by Satanic themes. They were just out to make some weird stuff. Police also said there were no reports of any devil worshipping at the Bulb. On any given day visitors will find souls no more threatening than joggers and parents pushing baby strollers.

But the images were so compelling, the setting so eerie, the location so close to the grisly discoveries of the bodies, that they were hard to ignore. In dramatic, made-for-TV-news form, the Bulb was intended to plant more seeds of reasonable doubt in the minds of potential jurors, who within months would be inundated with the prosecution's evidence at the preliminary hearing. It was typically bold and theatrical, typically Mark Geragos, as he pulled out all the stops to save Scott Peterson's liberty and, perhaps, his life.

The country hadn't gotten a good Satanic scare since the late 1980s with the Nightstalker case of Richard Ramirez, who treated a courtroom audience to a "Hail, Satan!" In the years between the Manson Family slayings and Ramirez, it seemed the country's criminal element was deep into black magic. Police departments had special occult units. Talk shows were full of lurid tales of Satan worshippers. Daycare workers facing charges of abusing children fell under suspicion of satanic motivations.

But the fears flamed out after Ramirez, the panic doused by the cold realities in study after study that found no evidence of widespread satanic cult crimes. By the early years of the new millennium, evil had a new face. And when the World Trade Center collapsed, it was international terrorism, not homegrown devil worship, that preoccupied the country.

But early in the Peterson case, black was back.

The cult theory evolved from the original, less-defined defense claim of Other People Out There. It would become a mantra. "I'm worried about, as the court well knows, trying to identify who I consider to be the real perpetrator of this crime," Geragos said at the June 5 hearing on the gag order, autopsy report and wiretap sanctions. At another hearing, co-counsel Matt Dalton said: "We have information that could possibly affect the arrest of other suspects who are still out there." Then, in July, Geragos told the court he had blockbuster evidence that "totally exonerates" Scott.

"The evidence, which demonstrates Mr. Peterson's innocence, also provides evidence of the true killer or killers' modus operandi and provides clues as to the method of and circumstances surrounding the killings," Geragos wrote in court papers. He added: "If the evidence is made public the ability of both the prosecution and defense to ascertain the identity of the actual perpetrator(s) will be irreparably prejudiced."

So who were these actual perpetrators? Police and prosecutors said they had no idea. Nobody was arrested and Scott remained imprisoned. The defense didn't give names, but it did offer some clues. In the June 2 issue of *People* magazine, under the headline, "The Satanic

Scenario," Geragos suggested that two things, a "mysterious van" and the disappearance of another pregnant woman whose body was found on the San Francisco Bay shoreline, may be linked to Laci's abduction and murder. He told the magazine that the days of the two women's disappearances—May 1 for the first woman and December 24 for Laci—were high holy days on the satanic calendar. "That's one scary picture of who's out there," he told *People*. In other reports, the defense would point to sightings of a man with a 666 tattoo seen in the area around the time of Laci's disappearance and suggest that the mystery van had satanic symbols on it.

Much of the defense's van theory seems to have stemmed from an incident outlined in a police report. Obtained by MSNBC, the report spoke of a woman claiming in December 2002 to have been lured into a brown Chevy or Ford van where two men and two women raped her "and a satanic ritual was conducted." The woman, who told this to a sexual assault counselor who then contacted police, also stated that during the ritual the other people mentioned a Christmas Day death that she would read about in the newspaper.

The other missing pregnant woman case referred to eight-months-pregnant Evelyn Hernandez, who, along with her 5-year-old son Alex, disappeared in the spring of 2002. Her body, or what was left of it—just the lower torso, still clad in maternity clothes—was found floating in San Francisco Bay on July 24, 2003, near a sea wall. Alex's body had not been found, though police presumed he was dead. The woman's remains were located far from where Laci was discovered—on the other side of the bay along the Embarcadero.

The women also came from different worlds.

Evelyn grew up poor in El Salvador and came to the United States when she was 14 years old. She lived with her mother and learned English. Her son Alex was born when Evelyn was 17 and unmarried. She finished high school and worked a number of jobs, including as a waitress, raising her son on her own, until, at age 24, she vanished.

Her family complained bitterly that Evelyn's case was ignored by the media because of her background and social status. Twenty people attended the memorial service for Evelyn; the choir alone was seven and a half times larger at Laci's memorial. At Evelyn's service a woman held up a sign with a picture of the child reading: "Where is Alex? Wasn't this investigation important?"

Scott Peterson's defense thought so. It considered the circumstances of Laci's and Evelyn's cases close enough to request police reports on the unsolved Hernandez case. In the words of defense attorney Kirk McAllister, this case could help find the "actual perpetrators" of Laci's murder.

The van and the Other Laci. It was provocative stuff. But could the defense prove they were linked to Laci?

In June, police announced they had found the van in question, towed it away to the state crime lab in Ripon and had it examined by criminalists.

They didn't find any evidence linking the vehicle to the murder of Laci Peterson or anybody else. What's more, several people whom the district attorney's office said were "associated with the van" were interviewed, and were "excluded from having any involvement in the disappearance of Laci Peterson," according to a DA statement.

"This is the second time they've been contacted and investigated by police during this investigation," the DA statement said. "It remains the position of this district attorney that this van was not involved in any way with the disappearance of Laci Peterson."

As for the Evelyn Hernandez case, the defense couldn't provide more evidence to bolster its theory because police simply wouldn't provide the evidence. Although San Francisco authorities had let Modesto police review the investigative files for Hernandez, they took the position that virtually everything in those files was off-limits to Scott Peterson's defense team. The defense fought it, but the judge agreed with the San Francisco authorities.

"I'm satisfied there is a considerable public interest in keeping it sealed," Judge Girolami said, in denying Peterson access to the five big binders of files during a July 9 hearing. The judge characterized as "highly speculative" any link between the two cases, and said the Hernandez investigation "is still ongoing and could easily be jeopardized if that material is made public and shared with other people."

The judge did, however, allow Scott's lawyers to see Evelyn Hernandez's autopsy report, though it made no mention of any satanic overtones to the death. In fact, like Laci's autopsy, there wasn't even a cause of death determined.

Evelyn Hernandez wasn't the only murdered woman case that would pique the defense's interest. In Boulder

City, Nevada, not far from Las Vegas, a woman walking her dog on a Monday morning in June 2003 saw body parts in a fishing pond in Veterans Park. The remains were identified as those of 49-year-old Boulder City resident Ladonna Milam, who worked as a porter in a hotel-casino near Hoover Dam. The last anybody knew about her movements, she had delivered towels to the room of Perry Carl Monroe of Alameda, California.

After police found packaging for a hacksaw and blades in Monroe's room, an arrest warrant was issued, and he was picked up a couple days later in Fresno when highway patrol officers found him sleeping in his car. A registration check turned up the murder warrant.

The case had many strange similarities to the Laci Peterson case, down to the suspect being caught in Amber Frey's hometown. It also had similarities to the Hernandez case. Las Vegas police touched bases with the Modesto police, and any thoughts Scott's defense had of uncovering a serial killer were diminished. Las Vegas police said they had no evidence linking the cases.

It wasn't the only setback for Scott's defense. Two other times, the court was unimpressed with the defense's other-killer or -killers theory. After defense attorney Dalton had claimed to have possible evidence of another killer, Judge Beauchesne indulged the defense in a secret hearing, at which they could lay out their cards. After the private hearing, Beauchesne said, "No evidence on the investigation of the 'other suspects' was presented."

Another time the other-killer scenario was raised came when Geragos tried to persuade the judge to keep the public from viewing the preliminary hearing. Geragos' argument was that the defense evidence to be aired at the hearing would be so incendiary it would tip off the real perpetrator. It is almost unheard of in California to hold a closed-door preliminary hearing, and the defense faced an enormous legal hurdle.

Predictably, this argument fizzled. Girolami ruled on August 14 that the hearing would proceed in open court, though without TV cameras. (The camera ruling had nothing to do with the defense's other-killer evidence; the judge was worried about hurting witnesses. The judge also rejected Geragos' claim that an open hearing would further poison the relatively small Stanislaus County jury pool. "Even considering that this is a capital case," the judge said, ". . . this court cannot make a blanket closure.")

There would be some other defense theories advanced with varying degrees of credibility. In a *People* magazine cover story in September, unidentified sources said that despite the DA's claims of "voluminous" evidence, the forensic evidence was slim. There was no blood or vomit found in the Peterson home, as the tabloids had reported. There was blood in Scott's pickup—as he had alluded to in the Diane Sawyer interview—but tests found it was his blood, not Laci's, *People* reported.

The magazine also highlighted a defense theory that Conner could have been born alive. As authorities announced at the time the baby was found, the boy appeared to be a full-term infant, with a gestation period of about thirty-five to thirty-eight weeks. A source told

People that Laci had gone in for a doctor's visit on December 23, the day before she disappeared and a sonogram showed that the fetus was estimated at thirty-one weeks along. Even allowing for the usual uncertainty with sonograms, a gap of four weeks is significant. Adding another wrinkle to the issue was a report just days later in *The Modesto Bee* in which Laci's doctor, James Y. K. Yip, denied that Laci had had a sonogram at all on December 23, saying that it was merely a routine prenatal visit. Her last sonogram, the *Bee* said, was in September.

Another defense theory raised eyebrows, not because it suggested Scott was totally innocent, but because it acknowledged he was no saint.

Once Amber Frey surfaced, the prosecution had a compelling motive for murder: eliminate Laci and run off with Amber, with $250,000 to sweeten the deal. To counter this, the defense would not try to destroy Amber's credibility, but embrace the affair by suggesting that Scott was quite the horn dog. It would tell the jury of at least a half-dozen women with whom he'd had romantic relationships after his marriage. Amber, according to what would be called the Cad Defense, was just the latest in a string of lovers—they only saw each other a few times—and hardly meant enough to Scott that he would kill his wife to be with her.

Perhaps the most compelling evidence the defense possessed didn't involve other women or sonograms or even Satan, but Scott's own friendly neighbors.

Even before Scott had his first court appearance, his parents were alluding to what would become a defense theme: a rush-to-judgment. "Chief [Roy] Wasden made a comment during his news conference that on the evening before Christmas Eve, Laci's mother had spoken to Laci at 8:15 and that's the last time anyone saw Laci," said Lee Peterson in the *Time* interview posted on the magazine's Web site. "Not true. There are several people who saw Laci."

Indeed, in the weeks after her disappearance, witnesses did come forward who corroborated key parts of Scott's story—that when he left the house at 9:30 a.m. on December 24, Laci was very much alive and ready to walk their golden retriever McKenzie. These witnesses, credible, upstanding citizens with no reason to lie, would later recount their stories in *The Modesto Bee* and other news outlets. Among them was Peterson neighbor Mike Chiavetta, a history teacher and water polo coach at Modesto High School, who recalled seeing a woman in a big white smock and black leggings—similar to the outfit that Scott said Laci was wearing the day she disappeared—walking a golden retriever in East La Loma Park around 10:45 a.m. Another witness, commercial painter Homer Maldonado, thought he saw Laci between 9:45 and 10 a.m. on December 24 about a half-mile away from the Peterson home. Finally, there was Vivian Mitchell, wife of three-term City Councilman Bill Mitchell, who said that as she was washing dishes on December 24 she looked out her window at about 10:15 a.m. and saw Laci, wearing black and white clothes, walking her dog down Buena Vista Avenue not far from Laci's house. "I had seen Laci walk by the house several times before," she told *The Modesto Bee*. "When she walked by on Christmas Eve, I hollered to Bill, 'Oh, look, it's the lady with the golden retriever.' "

In the interview with *Time* magazine, Scott Peterson's mother said that police tried to "discredit" some of these early witnesses. And, in fact, Homer Maldonado did say he filed his report about a week after the disappearance, but that officers told him the bloodhounds indicated that Laci had traveled a different route than Maldonado had indicated. He was not called back. And Vivian Mitchell said she called police about five days after Laci disappeared to report the sighting, but nobody ever called her back until her politically connected husband contacted the city manager.

There were still some problems with the so-called timeline witnesses. Some recalled the weather as being pleasant the day they saw Laci, but National Weather Service reports had it cold and cloudy. The prosecution would surely argue at trial that the witnesses were simply mistaken about the day they had seen Laci or had seen another pregnant woman that day. The neighborhood did seem to be full of expectant mothers—at least three, including one who not only looked like Laci, but who also walked a golden retriever. Still, authorities were sufficiently concerned about the so-called timeline evidence that they hypnotized one of the women, who was at about the same stage of pregnancy as Laci, to help jog her memory to see if she recalled walking her brown dog that day. The results of the hypnosis weren't revealed.

All of these theories, from the satanic cult to the timeline witnesses, tumbled forth in a relatively short amount of time—from April to August of 2003—as Scott's lawyers pored through a mountain of prosecution "discovery": police reports, investigator notes, witness statements, photographs, computer analyses and hundreds of hours of audiotaped phone conversations picked up by the wiretaps. It was a mad scramble to get through all this, plus work the public relations machine, while fighting off the gag order and trying to prepare for the preliminary hearing. That the defense was able to accomplish as much as it did in just four months was impressive.

Still, it was leaving Scott impatient.

He was never one to show much emotion in court. To be sure, most of the hearings were dry affairs in which lawyers argued over such things as the state and federal rules of wiretapping and the statutes applying to the unsealing of search warrant affidavits. The only time he seemed to lose composure was when the autopsy report was discussed at one of the first hearings. The rest of the time he would be impassive, bordering on the smug.

That changed on June 26 when his lawyers asked that the preliminary hearing, then set for July, be moved to September. At the time, the defense had the twin problem of having a mountain of prosecution discovery to go through, yet still waiting, frustrated, for the prosecution to deliver thousands more pages of documents, which were slower in coming because they were being sorted and labeled by the police.

Defendants are entitled to a speedy trial, and the judge must get their consent before agreeing to a delay, even one the defense itself asks for. It's a routine matter and the defendant just as routinely gives a simple, "Yes, Your Honor," when asked if he waives his right to a speedy trial.

Only this time, Scott wasn't going to make it routine.

When Gerolami asked if Scott agreed to the delay, Scott answered in a loud voice with an annoyed tone: "I think we are forced to without the information coming from the prosecution."

The judge asked him again so the record would be clear.

"It's not my wish," said Scott, "but yes."

A little over two months later, when the defense asked for yet another delay, the reality of the monumental task ahead seemed to sink in for Scott. There was no more annoyance, no more attitude, when the judge asked him at a September 2 hearing whether Scott agreed to a postponement of the preliminary hearing until October.

"I do, Your Honor," Scott said.

Scott wasn't the only one growing impatient with the course of the litigation. While he remained locked in jail, the bodies of his wife and son were locked in the offices of the Contra Costa County coroner's office. They spent four months there, and Laci's family was growing tired of waiting. The family wanted Laci and Conner to have a proper burial, so that the two beings at the center of this storm would at last rest in peace.

There would be nothing peaceful about what happened next. It was an attempt at closure that only opened more wounds, prompting allegations of a final betrayal in a saga that had seen more than its share of them.

CHAPTER 24

In the days after Laci Peterson disappeared, nobody was
more supportive of her family, of her husband, of the
case, than Brad Saltzman. The Red Lion Hotel manager
had donated space, phones, equipment and supplies for
the volunteer search center. He made rooms available
for news conferences. But more, he symbolized and em-
bodied the community spirit of Modesto. Even as the
case took a turn for the worse and suspicion fell on Scott
Peterson, Saltzman tried to stay above the fray, focusing
always on the search for Laci, of doing the right thing.
In the face of pressure from the community, Laci's family and his corporate bosses, he arranged for work space
for Scott's one-day search center in Los Angeles. It was
what friends did.

Then one night in May he was watching television.
Scott Peterson's father, Lee, was on *Larry King Live*
complaining about how Laci's family had broken into

the Covena house and hauled off all that stuff, singling out Laci's mother, Sharon Rocha, for criticism. "Instead of grieving," Lee said, "Sharon apparently planned this break-in."

Saltzman was disgusted.

Lee Peterson had just got his goat.

"I didn't understand how he couldn't have any compassion for her—not the kind of person that I want to sort of welcome, you know, with open arms and extend courtesies to," Saltzman told MSNBC's Dan Abrams.

So he didn't. When Scott's mother Jackie Peterson called a couple weeks later inquiring about a room at the Red Lion, Saltzman recommended they stay elsewhere.

"We weren't sold out," he told Abrams. "It was . . . my personal opinion, not the opinion of the ownership, but I felt like, you know, we've come so far in this and you've got to understand a little how Sharon is feeling. . . . I look at the hotel, Dan, almost as my house. And would I want to open up my home to someone with that type of attitude? The answer is no. So, I think it was pretty clear to them that they're really not welcome and I'd like to see them elsewhere."

If the winter of 2002 showed Modesto at its best, the summer of 2003 showed the town as something much different. The families of Scott and Laci, once united in the search for their brown-eyed girl, were now not only apart, but battling openly, each side consumed with its own sense of justice, its own grief. It was, to be sure, a difficult time. Laci and Conner, once the loving daughter and the grandson-to-be, had by now, due to the necessities of the legal system, slowly been dehumanized, reduced to evidence held in cold storage.

Evidence that Scott Peterson had a right to examine.

As heinous as it sounds, in any homicide case, some of the best, most revelatory evidence comes from the bodies of the deceased, often revealing everything from a medical determination of cause of death to the circumstances of the murder. The smallest nicks and cuts, trace evidence, the clothes—all can tell a story, and all can help convict or acquit. On August 14, lawyers for both sides entered into a stipulation granting Scott's defense team the go-ahead to pull Laci and Conner from storage and examine their remains.

According to the agreement, Geragos could bring in a radiologist to X-ray the remains. Up to four people for the defense, including scientific experts and the lawyers, would be allowed to watch. So, too, could up to two people chosen by the Stanislaus County District Attorney's Office, two coroner's officers to maintain chain of custody and a physician selected by the coroner.

On Monday, August 11, the defense contingent arrived at the coroner's office. The group included Geragos and his celebrity forensic scientists, Dr. Henry Lee, whose sharp criticism of the L.A. crime lab was instrumental in O. J. Simpson's acquittal, and Dr. Cyril Wecht, the Allegheny County, Pennsylvania, coroner and a frequent talking head on cable news shows. Prosecutor Dave Harris was on hand for the prosecution, as were Modesto police representatives. They stayed inside the criminalistics laboratory in Martinez for 2½ hours and emerged with only terse gag order–restricted comments.

"There's not much we can talk about," Geragos said—though the next day those same two forensic scientists would be observed by the *Modesto Bee* reporter being briefed by a defense lawyer on the satanic cult theory.

Under the stipulation, once the examination was completed, the coroner was "authorized to release the remains of Laci Peterson and the baby Conner Peterson to the next of kin." In this case, that was Laci's family, and in a statement from Sharon Rocha issued by one of their lawyers, Adam Steward, they urged attorneys and authorities to do just that.

These past eight months have been tremendously difficult for our family as we put so much hope and energy behind searching for Laci only to have our worst fears confirmed in April. There are no words to describe the pain we felt when we learned the remains were those of our beautiful daughter and unborn grandson. We have spent these past four months enduring this pain every day, every hour, every minute.

The events of this week have once again added pain to our daily grief as we read in the newspaper details regarding our daughter and grandson's remains and hear unnecessary graphic details when we turn on the television. We respectfully ask that all deliberate attention and effort be made by Mr. Geragos to return Laci and Conner to us. As the family, we plead with the media to be sensitive to the fact that this is not a media story to us. This is our Laci and Conner whom we love with all our hearts. This is not a story . . . this is our life.

Please treat her in death respectfully so that we as

her family will be allowed to lay her and Conner to rest in dignity and peace when the time comes. We ask that you respect our privacy and understand our pain as we grieve for our beautiful Laci and baby Conner.

On Thursday, August 21, the remains of Laci and Conner were delivered to the Stanislaus County Sheriff's Office, where they were kept while Laci's family made funeral arrangements.

On a warm Friday under blue skies, a white hearse carrying two caskets pulled into the Burwood Cemetery in Escalon. Unlike Laci's birthday memorial, this was a private service, with about 250 invited guests assembling on the green grass of the cemetery around the white canopy over the gravesite. The mourners had just arrived from a mass at St. Joseph's Catholic Church in Modesto, where the Reverend Joseph Illo spoke of grief, anger and forgiveness.

"I often ride my bike along the Dry Creek trail and would say a prayer for Laci last winter as I passed the shrine and banner set up at East La Loma Park," he said in his homily. "Those prayers have not gone unanswered, because we have Laci with us again. Not as we would have wanted, but in fact we are all here, and she is with us again, and God will take care of her."

He said that Laci "represented every daughter whose mother has had to bury her" and reminded people that "great evil can come at any time to the most beautiful of God's children."

"She, like many before her, even in this small city of Modesto, stands for our own aspirations and our own tragedies," he said. "Others have gone before her, and I see some of their parents with us today. Others will suffer after her. Thanking God for her life, we thank Him for our lives. Accepting her death, we accept our own." Even, he said, this "senseless death."

"Why did she and Conner die? What insanity drove the killer to destroy such beauty and such life? A young mother and her son," he said. "For this, there is no direct answer. I don't offer one, and neither do the Gospels. At His friend Lazarus' grave, Jesus did not explain death. He merely wept. . . . No one can undo her death, but we can allow Christ to redeem it by putting her death before His death on this altar, by pinning her eternity with His eternity in the Eucharist."

He found more parallels between her death and that of Christ's. "Lost on Christmas Eve, Laci became a carefully wrapped gift to be opened later; she and Conner portrayed the Mother and Child at the heart of the Christian mystery," he said. "Found on Good Friday, the day of Christ's death, her death is joined to that of her Savior. This remarkable timeframe—from Christmas to Easter—is certainly God's sign that the deaths of this mother and son were not meaningless, that Laci and Conner are with God. She was born with him in baptism, she suffered death with him, and she is raised with him in Christ. In Him we are reborn, in Him we live, and in Him we hope to die, so that we may be raised with Him. I ask all of you now to trust Jesus Christ; He went through this before Laci—He prepared the way for her, and He will take care of her."

He concluded by saying: "The word 'angel' in Greek means 'messenger,' messenger of God. We are all only human beings, not angels, but in a sense any one of us can be messengers of God, accomplishing His work. In that sense, as Laci lies before us, she speaks God's word from the other side of the grave. 'Do not fear death; fear only separation from God. I am with God—I am in His hands now.' Let us be good enough to listen carefully to this angel from the other side."

From there, the mourners went to the cemetery, where white doves were released.

And so was the anger.

"She was the light of my life," said her step-father, Ron Grantski, according to *The Modesto Bee*. "The animal that did this to her is going to pay."

For all the talk of angels and trust in Jesus, this sentiment was the bitter undercurrent.

Scott Peterson's parents were not invited to the funeral. They were not welcome at the inn, they were not welcome at the cemetery.

They had wanted to be there.

Jackie Peterson e-mailed Sharon Rocha to say so.

The past eight months fill the most difficult moments in all our lives. Arriving soon will be more trying times for all of us. We are dismayed at the failed efforts of Judge Giolami to close the coming hearing. Our effort to do so centered on keeping the press from exploiting the lives of Laci and Conner. Scott is brokenhearted over not being able to protect his family on that fateful day in December and now again not being able to protect the memories of Laci and Conner.

We are writing with an appeal to your heart. Though by law, you are granted the decision on how to handle the remains of all our loved ones, we ask you to postpone the service until such time as Scott is exonerated and we all join together as a family to mourn your daughter, Scott's wife, our and your grandson and Scott's son who has been taken from all of us so cruelly.

Please respond so that I know you received this. Our hearts go out to you and your family. We, as you, miss Laci every minute of every day. She had that effect on those close to her.

She got her response.

Jackie Peterson, who once received loving handwritten notes from her daughter-in-law, this time got a cold letter from Adam Stewart an attorney hired by Laci's family. The postscript in Laci's life had at last been written—by counsel for a family that wanted nothing to do with the parents of the man Laci once loved.

Dear Mr. and Mrs. Peterson,

You have been aware for several months that our firm represents the interests of the Rocha family. Despite this, you continue to contact members of the family and friends via e-mail, mail and telephone. We ask that you discontinue this practice immediately. The family wishes to be left alone during this difficult time.

Later, after the funeral from which she was barred, Jackie Peterson fumed. "It was unforgivable," she said. "If 250 people can attend, surely there's room for the grandparents of the baby." She said she, too, wanted some "finality."

Then Jackie Peterson spoke for Laci, the consummate hostess, the little Martha Stewart, the one who always knew what to do—what the right and proper thing was to do—in delicate situations just like this.

Once appearances meant so much. Now they meant nothing.

"Laci," Jackie Peterson said, "would have been appalled."

UPDATE: DECEMBER 2004

Mark Geragos, the attorney for Scott Peterson, faced jurors on Wednesday, June 2, 2004, in a Redwood City, California, courtroom and asked them to consider the things that weren't there—the blood, fibers, fingerprints and eyewitnesses the police couldn't find; the bags and boxes of items seized, collected and tested, the phone calls monitored, recorded and transcribed, the tracking devices affixed and activated, that all amounted to the same thing.

"Zip, nada," he said. This was the defense response to the prosecution scenario laid out the day before: that Scott cooked up a plan to kill pregnant wife Laci shortly after meeting—and falling for—Amber Frey, then carried out that plan by murdering Laci, dumping her body into San Francisco Bay, and conjuring a fishing alibi that stank worse than the sturgeon he never caught.

It was a strong presentation, looking all the better following the prosecution's long, rambling statement that offered few surprises. Geragos was at his best—forceful, funny, charming. He could have stopped right there with the classic reasonable doubt defense. But he didn't.

"Not only is Scott Peterson not guilty," said Geragos, "he's stone-cold innocent."

After an 11-day pretrial hearing in November 2003 in Modesto, Peterson was bound over for trial in Superior Court, appropriately moved to Redwood City, south of San Francisco, for a new judge and new jury pool—a change of venue that was a victory for the defense, which worried that Peterson couldn't get a fair trial in his hometown.

Before a six-man, six-woman jury that took a difficult two months to select, prosecutors unfurled an intricate, circumstantial case, one that offered no smoking-gun evidence; in fact, no murder weapon at all. Nor was there a compelling motive, and only little physical evidence. Rather, prosecutors David Harris and Rick Distaso focused on Scott's credibility and character, his words and actions—and his silences and inactions—before and after the murders, including the most damning testimony: his differing stories of what he did the morning of Laci's disappearance, telling some he was golfing, others fishing.

The state's marquee witness, Amber Frey, revealed no confession by Scott or any other direct evidence of his guilt. Rather, she spoke of their strawberry-and-champagne first date that ended in hotel sex—weeks before Laci disappeared. Confident on the stand, Frey painted a picture of Scott as the lying cad who, even after Laci disappeared, continued to call Amber, addressing her as "sweetie" and telling her, "We could fill each other, you know, forever."

That these calls came as volunteers were searching for Laci, that her family was crying over her loss, that a candlelight vigil was being held—that a city and a nation prayed for the pretty mom-to-be with the million-dollar smile—served as the most powerful evidence that not only could Scott Peterson lie, but that he could live a lie, comfortably. By the time the jury saw autopsy photos of Laci and baby Conner, barely recognizable as human beings, Scott's lies and amorous antics were seen in a colder, crueler light. Several jurors wept as the grisly pictures were projected on a big screen.

Still, it was an erratic start for the prosecution, punctuated by aggressive cross-examination grillings of police investigators over what the defense claimed was shoddy police work. But the state got a boost when prosecutor Birgit Fladager, a behind-the-scenes advisor, moved to the counsel table. Her clear, concise questioning of detective Craig Grogan helped piece together the jigsaw puzzle of a circumstantial case—and brought order, continuity and clarity to the presentation.

By the time Geragos called his own witnesses, some of his more provocative theories—including one that transients may have kidnapped and killed Laci, then tossed her body into a canal near San Francisco Bay—seemed increasingly far-fetched. In the end, the defense struggled to explain the most critical questions: Why did Scott give different alibis, and why did the bodies wash up at almost the exact location where Scott says he went fishing? By summations, Geragos couldn't live up to the expectations he himself had set by calling Scott "stone-cold innocent."

After 7½ hours of discussion, which had to be re-started after the departure of the first jury foreman, the hotel-sequestered jury reached a verdict.

On Friday, November 12, 2004, Scott Peterson was convicted of first-degree murder in the death of Laci, and second-degree murder in the death of Conner. The charges carried the special circumstance of multiple murder. Scott now faced a fate that authorities had been willing to bargain away so long ago when they had asked him to lead them to the bodies in exchange for not seeking the death penalty.

The penalty phase was, as expected, an emotionally grueling ordeal, as witnesses bared the ugly aftermath of murder. Laci's mother, Sharon Rocha, who once was so impressed by her son-in-law Scott, now stared him down and yelled: "Divorce is always an option! Not murder!" Scott's side called a staggering 39 witnesses of its own, ending with Geragos' pathetic appeal: "Just don't kill him. That's all I am asking of you. End this cycle."

On Monday, December 13, 2004, jurors decided that Scott Peterson should die by lethal injection. Afterwards, the jurors seemed tired, spent, but secure in their decisions. They spoke of the tedium, the pressures, the gruel-ing deliberations. And they spoke of Scott. Rarely did he show tears or remorse or even anger, they said. "At the end—the verdict—no emotion, no anything," said juror Richelle Nice. "That spoke one thousand words loud and clear."

They noticed the things that weren't there.